EARN MONEY in RETIREMENT

How to draw on a lifetime of experience to supplement your pension

Jim Green

howto books

Published by How To Books Ltd,
3 Newtec Place, Magdalen Road,
Oxford, OX4 1RE, United Kingdom
Tel: (01865) 793806 Fax: (01865) 248780
email: info@howtobooks.co.uk
http://www.howtobooks.co.uk

British Library Cataloguing in Publication Data
A catalogue record for this book is available from
the British Library.

Produced for How To Books by Deer Park Productions, Tavistock
Typeset by *specialist* publishing services ltd, Milton Keynes/Montgomery
Cover design by Baseline Arts Ltd, Oxford
Printed and bound by Cromwell Press Ltd, Trowbridge, Wiltshire

Note: The material contained in this book is set out in good
faith for general guidance and no liability can be accepted
for loss or expense incurred as a result of relying in particular
circumstances on statements made in the book. The laws and
regulations are complex and liable to change, and readers should
check the current position with the relevant authorities before
making personal arrangements.

Contents

Preface

When you retire from the workplace you continue to face the prospect of escalating living expenses: food, shelter, clothing, power supply, communications, insurances, council tax, etc., with less left over than you previously had at your disposal for enjoying the minor luxuries of life. And for the majority of retirees the prospect is doubly daunting as a direct result of vastly reduced incomings.

So what do you do; bite the bullet and settle for cutbacks in the quality of life?

Not inevitably so, because with tried and tested guidance, you can stretch your abilities to make some extra cash in retirement. For some this is not so much an option as a necessity.

This book focuses on providing the essential guidance by introducing you to ways and means of earning money in retirement in the traditional sense and, perhaps more significantly, in the new world of digital commerce which offers enterprising retirees a myriad of risk-free opportunities to create a steady flow of electronically-generated income. Follow the guidelines and you will make money. While you are unlikely to get rich whatever you do earn could represent the difference between coppering up every month to meet your commitments and looking at a surplus to spend or save as you wish.

In whichever direction you choose to travel, offline or online, you will not be left to your own devices because throughout this text you will find a multitude of links to resources designed to help you get the best out of earning in retirement and for your added convenience many of these links are repeated by category in the Appendix.

Good luck, and enjoy your retirement!

Jim Green

REVIEWING THE OPTIONS OFFLINE AND ONLINE

1
Turning retirement into profitable activity

When we become third age people it is vital to keep the mind firing on all cylinders if we are to be all we can be – and if this mental activity can be converted into profitable pursuits, so much the better. My book *Your Retirement Masterplan* (How To Books ISBN 1857039874) is devoted to the myriad elements that combine to make for a rewarding and fulfilling third age experience. This new book focuses exclusively on just one of these elements:

The evolvement of a money-making plan to add to the meagre income on which the majority of retirees struggle to subsist

We have choices:

1. We can conform to what the misguided still believe retirement is all about: doing nothing, wallowing in boredom, eating half the day, sleeping the other half, aging rapidly, and throwing off the mortal coil prematurely.

2. We can drift along and fritter away time and whatever income or savings we have at our disposal.

3. We can (if we have oodles of spare cash) indulge *ad nauseam* in perpetual vacationing.

or ...

4. We can apply ourselves to ensuring that our native abilities are kept alive, active, and sufficiently energised to augment the quality of life.

5. *We can stretch our abilities to make some extra cash in retirement.*

And for some, the final option isn't so much a choice as a necessity.

HOW DO WE GO ABOUT CREATING PROFITABLE ACTIVITY?

- Is it so restrictive that only a small number can succeed?
- Is it so demanding that only able-bodied retirees can make a go of it?
- Is it so difficult that only the super-intelligent stand a chance?

No, no, and no again – *anyone* can do it. If, for example, you are disabled or handicapped to some degree and would find it impossible to engage in a physical money-making activity you can still participate in 'online' enterprise – for which alternative route you will find many options in this book.

ENTREPRENEURSHIP AND THE RETIREE

You have reached or are approaching your 60th/65th year and are eligible for retirement. Or maybe you're only 50 and opted out early.

- Do you punch the air with a tightly clenched fist now that you have finally escaped from the workplace?
- Or do you ask yourself, 'What do I do now?'

For many retirees, lounging around the house or lying in the sun in a deck chair is not a prerequisite for third age enjoyment and fulfilment. While the world is undoubtedly aging and the number of elderly people is increasing, the current crop of senior citizens is in better health and lead longer, more active lives than their parents did. They want action, not eternal relaxation; excitement, not enforced leisure; accomplishment, not resignation.

Conventional retirement is just too dreary, and many remain emotionally unprepared to throw the working life concept entirely to the wind. Some could also make good use of opportunities to increase basic income.

So, in lieu of conventional retirement, a significant number of third age people are turning to entrepreneurship as an alternative. With valuable commercial skills acquired through years of practical experience, many of these retirees give serious consideration to launching their own businesses. They believe they still have what it takes and are highly motivated to succeed on their own.

HIGHLIGHTING THE ADVANTAGES

25-year-olds starting a business face different challenges from 50/60-something year-olds. It is not the same and there are distinct advantages open to relatively older entrepreneurs.

Prosperity and affluence

Retirement and the advancing years frequently indicate that the children of the family are all grown up and finished with education; the mortgage has been paid off; discretionary funds are at a higher level than ever before and, all in all, financial outgoings have considerably eased off. Economists reckon that the current crop of retiring baby boomers are economically more secure and enjoy higher income levels than past generations. *This is not so for every retiree, but for some.* If you are one of the lucky ones, then engaging in entrepreneurship may be your best option, but even if you have neither prosperity nor affluence to fall back on, the route is still open as you will discover as you course through the pages of this book.

Minimal financial risks

Older people are not as impatient or impetuous as the younger generation. With ample time on their hands, senior citizens can take as long as required to assess ideas, scrutinise the commercial concept, analyse market opportunities, develop saleable products, test novel market services, and prepare a feasible plan of enactment. They may even introduce business contacts from the past into the venture to add complementary expertise. As a result, they can significantly minimise financial risks.

Wealth of experience

One of the core benefits of participating in active retirement is the ability to draw freely on accumulated experience, and so it makes good sense to create an enterprise in an area related in some respect to your previous occupation. If you served in the Armed Forces you might consider setting up a venture as a supplier of military equipment and/or services under the auspices of a licence provided by the Ministry of Defence. If like me you worked at the sharp end of the marketing services industry you could write a how-to book based on your expertise or produce a series of instructional e-books to sell online. In point of fact, no matter what you did for a living, there are openings available to you in retirement for profitable activity in a field connected with your aggregated know-how.

In the chapters to follow you will come across dozens of such ideas, one of which might propel you in a profitable direction.

EVALUATING THE DRAWBACKS

As with any course of action in life there are drawbacks to engaging in entrepreneurship at a late age and it would be negligent to ignore their significance.

Your state of health

Health is a vital issue that you will need to address if you opt to forego a sedentary life in retirement. Entrepreneurship is a rigorous activity, not only physically but mentally. You will want to be certain that your health can cope with the demands and challenges of starting and running a business in the traditional sense. However, on a more optimistic note, these pressures can be eased dramatically if you choose the 'online' route to private enterprise (on which topic more, much more, later).

Your physical readiness

Even though you may be in good health, starting your own business can prove extremely arduous; an 'offline' start-up needs careful nurturing that may necessitate working long hours – particularly at the outset. Moreover, you will be subjected to stress as you lead your enterprise through all levels of profitability and growth. Are you up to the physical demands of running a traditional offline business operation?

Your capacity for risk-taking

Are you prepared to gamble? Risk-taking may sometimes entail losing money. Many retirees starting up in an offline business have neither the financial security of an annuity nor access to personal financial resources to sustain them until the profits start to kick in. With the little money you have at your disposal, are you prepared to risk it in a commercial venture with uncertain monetary outcome? Unlike the 25-year-old who flounders and sinks in the inexact pool of commerce, a 60-year-old will have few opportunities to obtain gainful employment and start saving all over again for a replacement retirement nest egg. The third age is already staring you in the face. If you don't have assets to fall back on if you fail, then you ought to think twice about starting up on your own in the offline world. Or at least, use only a small part of your savings. Committing your entire resources to a business in retirement is not only too great a risk to take, it is sheer folly.

Your capacity and willingness to learn new skills

As a third age entrepreneur you must be capable of grasping and understanding new methods of doing things. Technology is changing the way business is done. You may not want to learn the new technology but you need to understand what it can do for you. You also need to know how to deal with younger people who will in the main be the people with whom you will be negotiating and cutting deals. Learning these new skills is absolutely vital if you opt to pursue profitable retirement activity online.

Although I participate in both options (often in tandem) you may have gained an early impression that my preferred route to profitable activity in retirement is online as opposed to offline. However, some retirees would disagree with me, and so we will cover both spectrums of opportunity in this book.

SO WHAT'S ON OFFER FOR THE ENTERPRISING RETIREE?

In Chapters 2 to 13 we will examine the available options; offline and online; from wood carving and embroidery to creating a multi-page website fully enabled for e-commerce or a modest one-page site designed to pull in orders; what you must learn to make an opportunity work for you; how to do it in practice; how to create income streams to add to your retirement earnings – and how to get a lot of fun out of managing your chosen enterprise.

Bear in mind that the majority of the suggestions reviewed are for part-time ventures that you can use as an *add-on* to your overall spectrum of retirement interests. They are not intended to take over your life or have you prepare a bulging business plan for funding purposes. Most of them (especially the online options) can be started and operated on a shoestring budget.

Let's go … it's not as difficult as you may think.

2
Making your lifetime knowledge work for you

You are a walking compendium of learned life skills; not just those skills you acquired in your career but the aggregated knowledge of a lifetime: work, hobbies, general interests, specialist interests, child bearing/raising/educating, and so on. The list is endless. And in one or more of these areas you are an expert.

You don't believe me? Then take a test and prove it for yourself.

1. Make a list in random order of topics that interest you.

2. Identify the one topic you instinctively feel you know more about than any of the others. Start jotting down in tabular form every aspect relating to your *conscious* knowledge of the topic as it springs to mind; one word per aspect will suffice. Keep on adding as the thoughts tumble out.

3. Repeat this exercise for the next topic in order of perceived interest.

4. Repeat it for the next again.

5. Leave your lists aside and come back to them a few days later.

Unless you are brain dead something has been occurring in the interim. Your little exercise has sparked off the interest of your subconscious and it is enthused about the outcome. It has been carrying this stuff around for years and is desperate to disclose the extent of your collective intelligence, to tell you how much you *really* know. Given the opportunity, it could have conveyed this information a long time ago.

But you never asked – until now.

Review each of your lists again individually and at the prompting of the second level of your consciousness keep on adding until you have exhausted the deepest recesses of your memory bank. Upon completion you may be shocked to discover that the topic you thought you knew most about is in fact the one about which you know the least. One of the others may have grabbed the Number One Spot thanks to the power of your subconscious.

There's enough information on the winning topic to write a book, right?

WRITING A BOOK ON YOUR KNOW-HOW

I've done it several times over; it's fun, it's therapeutic, and it can lead to streams of residual income if you do it correctly. The subject matter doesn't have to be related to what you did for a living. Perhaps a hobby interest came top of your list of 'expert' topics; perhaps it was something else that took you completely by surprise when you realised just how much you know about the subject. It makes no difference. If you are interested, other people are too, and they will want to know what you know.

WHAT YOU MUST DO TO MAKE YOUR PROJECT A REALITY

1. Lay out what you know about your specialist topic on a sheet (or several sheets) of paper. Start with headings for each element then beef up the text accordingly.

2. Explain in a paragraph or two the gist, why you are interested, and what you have derived from your accumulated intelligence gathering over the years.

3. Explain the mechanics of participation (features).

4. Explain what others would gain from learning what you know (benefits).

You do 1–4 above to fire up your resolve for the next stage ...

1. Compile a list of what you *do not know* about your topic.

2. Establish how you will rectify the shortfall in your knowledge (online research, reference library, other books on the subject, etc.)

3. Make a start on your researches and stick with them until you have gleaned what you still need to know.

4. You will be creating a work of non-fiction but you must decide on a category. Is it to be niche, ultra-niche, how-to, self-help – or what?

5. Identify your category and study everything associated with it: authors, publishers, writing styles, accepted formatting, market sub-sectors, etc. Visit bookstores and libraries; use the internet and reference manuals for your desk research.

6. From your researches select the publishing house most closely associated with producing books related in one way or another to your particular project.

7. Write to them requesting a copy of their 'author guidelines' or check their websites.

8. Study this material assiduously to get a feel for their stipulations.

9. Read several of the chosen publisher's listed books on similar subjects. Observe how authors craft titles, chapter headings, subheads, sub-subheads; how they employ bullet points and italics for emphasis. Determine the word count per page, per chapter, per entire book.

10. List all competitive titles on sale (the more the better because that will indicate a healthy market for your topic).

Get set for the third stage ... the creative process

Be honest with yourself right at the very start.

1. Are you capable of handling this project?

2. Is your vocabulary up to scratch?

3. Do you have reservations about grammar, syntax, etc.?

4. Get to work immediately on any areas of concern, and if that does not appeal to you, ditch the project. You won't be published unless the essence of your work is of the highest calibre and the command of your native tongue impeccable.

And now down to the nitty-gritty ...

Compare the writing of your book to that of the task facing an artist painting a landscape. The artist envisages in advance the composition of the picture (your list of contents), makes rough sketches of essential features (your draft copy) and arrives at a balanced decision on execution. The artist has choices on technique for implementation and so do you.

Why you should do this before you write anything

When you work away conscientiously on compiling the list of contents in advance, you open the door to choices on how you will tackle the actual writing of your book. Authors exercise preferences on execution. Some start at the beginning and continue right to the end without diversion; others tend to cherry pick, darting back and forth from one chapter or section to another. A few authors manage to combine both techniques successfully: while maintaining regular progress, they make the occasional detour as and when inspiration strikes.

Whichever route you decide to travel you'll need a reliable road map and that is why you should always compile your list of contents before you write a single word.

Matching the sequence to your research findings

As with any list of things-to-do, you begin compilation of the list of contents at the start, progress through the middle by highlighting all of the essential elements and end up at the end; the climax; the promise of fulfilment. To do this effectively, you must match what you know with what you have discovered and merge your accumulated findings into a logical sequence of factual information. Sounds easy, but you won't get it right first time. You just keep at it until everything clicks into place. You will know when that happens.

Now you can make a start on the first draft

Develop your own distinctive writing style. It's easier then you may imagine. Just talk to the reader as if he/she was sitting opposite you face to face – just as I am talking to you right now. You can't see me but you *hear* me just as you would if I was right there in front of you. Some experienced authors produce one draft chapter, review it, rewrite it – or discard it and start all over again. When satisfied they move on to a second chapter and repeat the process. I don't. I write the entire book in one fell swoop and I do so with confidence because I have my thoroughly researched, sequentially structured list of definitive contents to guide me all along the way. Then and only then do I undertake rewrites as required.

Above all, look upon the creative writing process as a joyous celebration, not a painful chore. Books created under duress invariably relay the writer's tension to the unfortunate reader.

And lastly, when you're happy with the final text ...

- Make a start on your proposal for publication. Study everything you can lay your hands on relating to this – including my tutorial *Secrets to Churning Out Bestsellers* (see website details below). The proposal is every bit as important as your text so treat its composition with equal diligence. It must include a synopsis, the list of contents, your target market, detailed marketplace analysis, major competitive titles, and your qualifications for writing the book.

- Choose your strongest chapter and use it as a sample to include with the proposal.

- Write your covering letter.

You might get lucky as I did with your very first proposal, or you may need to rethink your strategy, but if you follow the suggestions outlined above you will cut down considerably on the painful prospect of outright rejection.

> ## TIP
>
> Visit www.writing-for-profit.com and draw down a copy of my free taster *Everyone Has at Least One Book in Them*. It will provide you with a solid introduction to what we have just been discussing.

writing-for-profit.com

Writing for Profit: My Free eBook Shows You How to Get Started!

Home
FREE eBook
Money Makers
My New Titles
Download Tutorial
Hot News!
Testimonials
Residuals
Resources
Contact
Government Grants
What's This?
Find This?
Tutorial Contents
Realization

When you download this free Writing for Profit eBook you will be opening the gateway to getting started on a career as a purveyor of niche non-fiction – full time or part time as you wish. This introduction to my creative writing course will show you how writing for profit enables you to make money writing based on topics culled from your own extra income ideas. It will spark off inspiration to earn extra income at home by creating residual income streams.

Fig. 1. *Everyone Has at Least One Book in Them.*

CONSIDERING THE ELECTRONIC ALTERNATIVE

If attempting to have your book published in the traditional manner sounds like too much trouble you might want to consider the electronic alternative. *Convert your know-how into a series of digital tutorials, build a website, and sell them as e-books online.* This is a very fulfilling retirement pursuit which we'll be examining in greater detail when we arrive at Chapter 23.

SO, YOU DON'T WANT TO WRITE A BOOK?

That's okay. Use what you've just learned about your latent expertise to lay the foundations for a profitable retirement pursuit in the shape of a business, a product or service.

Adapting your expertise for commercial exploitation

To adapt your expertise for commercial purposes you follow a path similar to that outlined above for writing a book.

- Get it all down on paper.
- Explain the methodology.
- List the features.
- Highlight the benefits.
- Establish what you don't know about your topic.
- Rectify the information shortfall by researching.
- Stick with the research until you've located all you still need to learn.
- Identify your market.
- Find out how to reach it.
- Develop your business idea, product or service.
- Test-market.
- Promote.

As for the rest of it, that's the subject matter of the 31 chapters to follow …

3
How to create your own money-making ideas

There are countless ways in which you can use your latent expertise to start a profitable retirement pursuit. You might have a hobby out of which you could squeeze some additional income – or you could look at what other retirees are doing successfully and determine whether you could emulate their approach or develop it into a money-making idea of your own.

GO ONLINE FOR INITIAL RESEARCH

Literally thousands of amazing ideas are floating around out there in cyberspace just waiting to be tapped for free. Some of them are wacky, others workable as they stand, and some capable of individual development. Use Google.com – the best search engine of them all. Employ keyword phrases such as 'hobby ideas', 'retirement hobby ideas', 'business ideas', 'retirement business ideas', 'profitable retirement business ideas'; then try again by prefixing each of these search terms with the word '*free*'. You will uncover enough leads to keep you occupied for the next fortnight. Be selective though and you will save on time and undue stress. You'll soon get the hang of it and be able to recognise the more likely opportunities rapidly.

CONVERTING HOBBIES INTO RETIREMENT EARNERS

Hobbies feature prominently on the list of preferred activities for the majority of retirees. But what if you could convert your hobby into an

16

earner? Wouldn't that add to overall satisfaction? While not every hobby interest has the propensity to generate cash and some are no more than pleasurable pastimes; others have a commercial aspect attached if you dig deep enough to find it, and it is to a sample of these that we will give our attention shortly. This review may help you establish whether your own hobby has income generating possibilities – and if you don't have any hobbies, maybe you will locate one in your researches.

MAKING MONEY FROM WHAT YOU LOVE DOING

Using a hobby or favourite pastime as your part-time retirement business base has inherent benefits. Why do I say this? Because any venture you decide to become involved in should be something you love doing – something you believe in – something that you would work at no matter what income it would generate. This will give you the stamina to see your venture through dull times in the beginning and happier times later when there the profits start rolling in. We all know the feeling of doing something we hate. We can't give it 100 per cent enthusiastic effort and so we tend to not see it through. That's why it is vitally important to dearly love the concept you have chosen to build your profitable retirement pursuit around.

Do you like cooking?

Start a recipe newsletter for others who are interested in the culinary arts and sell your recipes by publishing a simple booklet. You could also produce a digital version and make it available as a download on the internet. (Read Chapter 23 on how to go about that.)

Do you enjoy crafts?

Sell the produce through mail order but be sure to mark up the price to cover shipping and handling charges.

Do you enjoy working on cars?

Print and distribute flyers around the local neighbourhood listing your prices. Offer a discount coupon for customers to use on their first auto repair job.

Do you enjoy computer programming?

Write a program and sell it through shareware groups or online to computer owners.

Just about anything you love doing can be magically transformed into a commercial opportunity. Some products and services may only sell in your own locality while others might do well in mail order or online if they are capable of digital conversion. As with any hobby, it will take time (probably many months) to realise a profit but think of it this way: most people who have a hobby know they have to spend money to participate. It only makes sense to promote your hobby to other like-minded enthusiasts so you can eventually make some of that money back in sales.

TEN POPULAR RETIREMENT HOBBY EARNERS

Artificial Flowers

You could earn some pin money from this hobby because of the ever growing demand from local retailers everywhere who use the produce to add ambience to their outlets. Make them up from special papers, ribbons, fabrics, buttons and beads – even shells – and include a selection of artificial pot plants for exterior display.

Candle Making

Candle making is enjoying a burgeoning popularity as a fine craft and as a retiree hobby. Only a few simple materials and tools are required to make your own handsome candles. Approach gift shops and market traders with samples of your produce but only sell to them on a margin that nets you at least 30 per cent profit.

Collecting and Antiques

Collector Online's club directory www.CollectorOnline.com is the most complete listing on collectors' clubs. Using the search facility is easy – just click on the letter you want to search and check the listings for clubs. It was at this website I discovered that a football medal I had acquired in my youth is now a collectable worth several hundred pounds. You might consider using eBay (see Chapter 11) as a sales channel for valuables you locate with this retirement pursuit.

Jewellery Making

This hobby can be confined to a relatively small space and requires no great outlay of money for tools and materials. It is wise, however, to work with a teacher at the beginning since there are tricks to soldering, setting stones and working with metal. Jewellery making is a potentially good income-producer for the enthusiastic retiree. Your marketplace is once again local gift shops and market traders.

Macramé

With a little string, you can make key rings or belts; with a lot, you can make planters or wall hangings. Another retirement hobby you could turn into a money spinner by calling on local retailers to make a presentation of your produce.

Pottery and Ceramics

Creating something from the raw earth, experimenting with shape and colour. This hobby is enormously satisfying: consequently, pottery making is one of the fastest-growing retirement crafts and the produce is a popular line with speciality stores.

Sewing, Knitting, Crocheting and Weaving

As pastimes, these handicrafts have the virtue of being readily started and stopped as time permits. As moneymakers, they are somewhat limited by competition, but if you enquire around you'll find some local market traders willing to handle your produce.

Winemaking

With experience you can attempt to reproduce the characteristics you find most desirable in fine vintage wines. A good wine-tasting class usually precedes interest in this hobby. You won't become another *Victoria Wines*, but you could build up a regular clientele among friends, colleagues, neighbours and wine enthusiasts.

Woodworking

Here's another choice that has income-producing potential since skilled woodworkers, carpenters, and furniture restorers are much in demand. Set up as a freelancer serving trade and public alike.

Writing

Do you have the urge to write a novel, short stories, poems – or a self-help book? Perhaps you have always wanted to try your hand at journalism. The web is a major source of advice on writing and research resources. Visit the *Writers' Exchange* website at www.writersdigest.com for extensive links to other writing sites and a writing community for sharing ideas. Then do as I do: combine offline and online to achieve results for your profitable retirement pursuit.

ROLLING OUT OPPORTUNITIES FROM OTHER PEOPLE'S IDEAS

It isn't the billions of ideas that pop up in the minds of humans around the globe that make money. Very few of them are worth the time it took to generate. Most ideas are fleeting sparks that go nowhere and are soon forgotten. Of the ideas that are good, very few are followed up and become worthwhile developments in the marketplace. Most people are just not orientated to do anything, while others believe it would take too much of their time and money to follow through to completion. This leaves the marketplace wide open for retirees who learn how to roll out opportunities from other people's ideas.

There are three major approaches you can use:

1. Find something that already exists, the presence of which isn't common knowledge.

2. Invent something. Most inventions are merely new arrangements of things that have already been created.

3. Alter or improve in any number of different ways something that already exists.

As you create ideas, write them down. What you dream up can be your key to a profitable retirement pursuit. Keep your mind open as you go through each day. What did you notice in the department store that would reduce costs, save money or increase sales if some simple procedure were added or something changed? Ideas for improvements are among the most valuable things you can contribute to society and at the same time add to your bank account. To create ideas for improvements, consider every possibility and alternative for the thing you want to improve.

Learn to create ideas by evaluating all the different aspects of the product, methodology or concept you are interested in. Put your imagination and subconscious to work and write down your thoughts about each of the things you expect to improve. Use the wealth idea format below as your guide for creating money-making improvements.

IDEA FORMAT: LIST THE THINGS YOU WANT TO IMPROVE

1. Why should it be improved?

2. Who will benefit from the improvement?

3. What is wrong with it at the present time?

4. Did someone else cause a problem with it?

5. How do you propose to improve it?

6. Do you have the facilities to do the work required?

7. Do you have the know-how to do the work required to improve it?

8. Exactly what part needs to be improved?

9. Should it be smaller? Larger?

10. Should the colour be different?

11. Would more activity help make it better?

12. Could it be combined with something else to make it more practical?

13. Would a different basic material work better?

14. Is it too complicated, could it be simplified?

15. Would a substitute be more meaningful?

16. Is it priced too high?

17. Can the shape be changed to advantage?

18. Can a new marketing plan make the difference?

19. Is it safe?

20. Can it be mass produced to bring the unit cost down?

21. Should the appearance be changed or streamlined?

22. Is there an adequate guarantee?

23. What can make it appeal to a bigger audience?

24. Would new packaging or a novel product name enhance
25. Can it be made heavier, lighter, higher or lower?
26. Can it be franchised?
27. Is there a good maintenance programme to back it up?
28. Can financing be simplified?
29. List ways to increase production.
30. List ways to increase sales.
31. List ways to reduce costs.
32. List ways to increase efficiency.
33. List ways to improve quality and increase profits.
34. What can be done with it to satisfy more people?

This format will start the ideas sparking and as related notions come to mind write them down in every variation you can think of. Do not judge the good or bad points of the ideas as they materialise, just write them down and judge them afterwards. You will stop the flow of ideas if you are critical of your thoughts before you put them on paper. When you have answered everything you can about the product or concept and know how it fits in with your plans, sit down and evaluate all the details you have written.

After you have found (or created) a good idea, follow it up with questions on what should be your next move in order to do something about it, then act; get it moving. Expose it to the world with sufficient tests to determine the value.

Come up with ideas that are still in the processing stage rather than get stuck on several vague points that can be worked out later as your subconscious goes to work. If your idea fails, it doesn't matter; you are just that much closer to finalising another one, then another, until a useful more valuable idea is born. Every manufacturing plant, retailer, solicitor, accountant; every business person, large or small, cannot continue to operate in the competitive world of today without someone in the organisation constantly coming up with new and better ideas.

Old ideas drop by the wayside as new ideas take their place. Old companies without new ideas fade away. Those who learn and know how to create ideas and anticipate the changes needed, as the future evolves, have the opportunity to be a great success with big money-making potential – even in retirement ...

Using intuition to find your money-making retirement pursuit

Another tool you can use to help dream up profitable ideas is to spend several minutes each evening, relaxed with your eyes closed. Pick any object that comes to mind and imagine changing it. Change it in every way you can think of to improve it. The following evening pick another subject or object and repeat the process. Soon you will be using 20 per cent of your brain power instead of the 10 per cent normally used by the average person. As your knowledge and brain power increase so will your bank account in retirement.

Just think what you could accomplish if you could get the other 80 per cent of your brain power working. On second thoughts, don't aim for 100 per cent efficiency – you'll probably wind up revolutionising the world!

PROTECTING YOUR IDEAS

When you have come up with a really good idea, write a full description of it and make a sketch if necessary. Put the written information, the sketch, and any other pertinent facts or documents in a self-addressed envelope. Have the post office seal the envelope with a date stamp over the flap then send it to back to yourself by registered mail. Keep the envelope, unopened, in the event you need to prove ownership. Of course if your product has a properly registered trade mark, has been copyrighted, or you have a patent, you are already protected from infringement.

SPARKING OFF MORE IDEAS

Another good way to spark off ideas is to go through the classified and wanted advertisements in the local newspaper – also the *Yellow Pages*. As you read, think of something that would be of value to prospective buyers, or enhance the item you are reading about.

PRACTISE OBSERVING EVERYDAY THINGS AND DETAILS

In summary, learn to develop ideas from observing everyday things and details. Think of what could make something that already exists better. Dwell on things that have a large marketing audience, something that everyone needs or wants. Write your ideas down. Put a pencil and pad at your bedside. When you remember a good dream, don't just lie there, because by morning you will forget it. Jot it down on the pad. You will be surprised what you can dream up. Maybe an idea for an ultra-profitable retirement pursuit will magically appear on your pad tomorrow morning …

WACKY IDEAS THAT CONSISTENTLY MAKE MONEY

Some people use far-fetched, off the wall ideas to make money online and a review of these might just help you locate your own wacky but profitable retirement pursuit.

Here are six examples to start you off:

Origami Boulders

Some say www.origamiboulder.com is pure genius. Whatever your opinion, there's no doubt this is a madcap idea which seems to be making sales. The site is set up like a spoof of sorts. This businessman sells an 'origami boulder' which is basically a screwed up piece of paper (the products come in a couple of different guises).

For $3 (approx. £1.60) the owner of this business will crumple up a 'boulder', throw it in the rubbish bin and email you with a description. He calls it performance art and an excerpt of the site's clever copy gives the flavour of this unusual business idea ... 'You place an order and get origami boulder artwork with a special card to display at your home or workplace – makes an unforgettable gift for friends!'

No sales figures are available, yet people do order his product. A deluxe kit is even available – crumpled-up paper on a bamboo platform. Check it out at www.origamiboulder.com.

Rent-A-Cow

Cheese lovers can rent their very own cheese maker – a brown-and-white cow living on a Swiss mountain. Dairy farmer Paul Wyler offers his cows for rent on the internet, with all the cheese they produce going to the 'virtual' owner. Cows cost around $280 (approx. £162) for the summer and Wyler looks after the animals and makes cheese from their milk. Renters can check photographs of the animals at Wyler's website before they pay up.

He and his wife Helga run a 50-head farm in the Brienz area of the Bernese Oberland. They already rent some of the cows to restaurants and say they came up with their Rent-a-Cow idea because they could not sell as much cheese as they produce every year. See www.kuhleasing.ch.

Filtering Flatulence

A Texas inventor has come to the rescue of those unfortunates afflicted with excessive wind. The 'Flatulence Filter' is an attractive chair-cushion air filter that puts an end to the embarrassing moments when nature quietly – or noisily – slips by. Frank Lathrop developed severe problems with intestinal wind as a result of his diabetes several years ago. His wife, family and the women he worked with complained about the odour caused by his problem, and so Lathrop decided to fix their dilemma himself. After almost two years of development the Flatulence Filter Seat Cushion was complete. Now manufactured and marketed by UltraTech Products Inc as the 'First Air Filter Disguised as a Seat Cushion', the special pad is 15" x 17" x 1" thick and looks like any normal seat cushion.

The air treatment system employs a carbon air filter that absorbs the flatulence odour. This same filtration technology purified the air breathed by the astronauts in the Space Shuttle programme and was used in the soldiers' gas masks during the Gulf War. The cushion sells for $39.95 (approx. £22) and is designed to absorb odours for 6–12 months. To date business has been brisk. The company also sells a flatulence filter pad which sufferers wear inside their underwear. Check out www.227unusualbusinessideas.com/weirdIdeas.

Act Rich with Phony ATM Receipts

Here's a truly crazy idea – phony ATM receipts. Would you believe there's a market for them? Fake ATM receipts can be used for messages written on the reverse or left on coffee tables to impress friends, during negotiations with mortgage companies, or in front of the *maître d'* at swish restaurants. The receipts show a fake balance of in excess of $350,000 (approx. £195,000) and can be purchased in packs of four for $3.99 (approx. £2.20) each! Look at www.227unusualbusinessideas.com.

Goggles for Dogs

The inventors of Doggles – sunglasses designed especially for dogs – say they came up with their business brainwave after noticing their dog was squinting in the sunlight. Ken and Roni di Lullo of MidKnight Creations tried their own glasses on their dog's face but nothing stayed put. After experimenting with sports goggles, the innovative husband and wife team developed a special pair to fit their dog perfectly. Other dog owners approached the couple when they were all out walking, and a business was born. After a story on Doggles featured on CNN, sales quadrupled overnight and these days the di Lullo's have a $1 million business. Check out www.doggles.com.

Bachelor Buttons

One may look at a thriving laundry, take stock of the machinery, note the number of hired helpers, and come to the conclusion that it took plenty of cash to start this small business. But that is not necessarily the case. A public stenographer couldn't make ends meet on her miserly earnings. She did some mending and a bit of laundering for her male patrons. The business soon began to grow and another pair of hands had to be employed. The enterprising young lady called her business 'The Bachelor's Laundry' and within 2 years handled over 100,000 bundles yearly, serving over 3,500 patrons. Laundry and mending is for male patrons only. Three trucks deliver the laundry daily. There is no extra charge for repairs.

In their book *227 Unusual Business Ideas* Ross Stokes and Kathy Crockett go the whole hog in their search for weird concepts that work-at-home entrepreneurs use to make money consistently. You can purchase it for $25.75 (approx. £14.30) at this website www.227unusualbusinessideas.com. It comes with a free companion volume *The Brainstorming Guide* to assist in developing your own unusual ideas.

BEFORE YOU START DEVELOPING YOUR OWN UNUSUAL IDEAS

Think about this …

- The biggest breakthrough for fast-food restaurants came from a bank. The drive-through window is just like a bank teller's window that opens outside. Perfect for picking up fast-food from your car.

- Slot machines date back to 100BC. They were used for dispensing holy water.

- *Kleenex* tissues were originally designed as make-up removers, until customers pointed out they were also ideal for nose-blowing.

- Did you know that one of the 'necessities' of modern life – the roll-on deodorant – was inspired by ballpoint pens?

- And who would have guessed that the whole science of fibre optics came about because of aerospace research, not because of the telecommunications companies which now use the technology daily.

Ideas are the lifeblood of any business, whether you're running a small home-based business or a large multi-national. So entrepreneurs are always on the lookout for places they can search for *new* business ideas.

When you borrow ideas, successful processes and unique selling points from other industries, you're simply doing what great thinkers have always done. You're broadening your mind, making yourself more receptive to new ideas and inputs. Looking, listening and thinking about a broad range of industries and businesses opens your mind to new possibilities for your own business opportunity.

4
Creating residual income streams

Creating residual income streams is not an impossible dream for those retirees charged with an entrepreneurial streak. Certainly to achieve manifold success offline is a challenge that may be beyond the majority, but the opportunity to do so online is open to every third age traveller. *Residual income* (also known as passive or recurring income) is income that continues to be generated after the initial effort has been expended. In other words, you do something once and it continues to generate income, perhaps for years on end. Compare this to how most people focus on earning: *linear income*, which is one-shot compensation or payment in the form of a fee, wage, commission or salary. Linear income is directly proportional to the number of hours invested in it (40 hours of pay for 40 hours of work) but one of the great advantages of residual income is that once things are set in motion, you continue making money from your initial efforts, while gaining time to devote to other things – such as generating more streams of residual income.

WHY CREATING RESIDUAL INCOME OFFLINE IS RESTRICTIVE

Offline opportunities are few because they are usually linked to special skills. Take writing for example. You put pen to paper and produce a book, the proposal for which is accepted for publication. You may be lucky enough to obtain an advance but here is how your residual income opportunity really starts to take shape. When your book is published the royalties from home, export and online sales will come in at around 7.5 to 10 per cent. Say it quickly and it doesn't sound like much but these basic royalties soon mount up to provide you with a handsome return year after year. When you start to hit reprints and multiple editions it gets even better and that's when your residual income opportunity takes off:

- Editions licensed to another publisher.

- Single issue or periodical rights.

- Translation rights.

- Sound broadcasting rights.

- Merchandising rights.

- Educational reprint rights.

- Royalty-inclusive sales.

- Mail order sales.

- Book clubs.

- PLR (public lending right: libraries).

Other ways to generate residual income offline where there is either a skill or discretionary funds to be tapped include:

- Transfer the rights to a software program you created or a gadget you invented to a company that agrees to pay you a percentage of each copy of your work sold in the future.

- Become an actor and draw residual income from each of your movies, TV shows, or commercials, each time they run.

- Allow an oil company to drill a well on your property in exchange for a percentage of the revenue.

- Purchase an office building or other commercial property that earns you recurring income through lease or rental payments.

- Start a savings and investment programme that pays you residual income in the form of interest or dividends.

The problem is that all of the opportunities discussed above call for highly specialised skills which the majority of retirees do not possess and that is why it is best to look online for opportunities.

WHY THERE ARE MORE OPPORTUNITIES ONLINE

The virtual nature of the internet makes it easier for anyone with a home computer (or access to one on a regular basis) to create streams of potential residual income online. The purpose of this book is not to introduce you to get-rich-quick schemes (you'll get your fingers burned rapidly if you follow that route) but to show you how with a little effort and patience you can participate in a myriad of legitimate ways to add to your retirement income. You don't have to be a wizard, a magician, or a geek. All you need do is to follow the instructions detailed in Chapters 7 to 33 and you will discover how to tap into residual streams by providing other internet users with what they want (not necessarily *need*).

WHY COUNTLESS MILLIONS ARE HOOKED ON THE INTERNET

People around the world use the internet for all sorts of reasons, but one specific reason consistently stands head and shoulders above all the others according to findings emanating from Forrester Surveys (the internet research arm): *information*. Everyone wants it, they want it instantly, and they want it for free. So how does that help us in retirement to carve out residual income opportunities? Online users can't always find what they want for free and even when they do it's often out of date, flawed, misleading, or worse still, useless. This opens up a gap into which part-time online marketers can step with information produce and software that is up to date, unflawed and useful.

'There you go again,' can I hear you say? 'I don't want to write information packages and I don't know anything about producing software'. That's okay. You don't have to produce your own (better if you can, though, as you'll find out shortly), because there are thousands of purveyors who'll gladly cut you in on a slice of the action if you promote theirs.

MARKETING YOUR OWN INFORMATION PRODUCTS

Self-publishing your own personally generated information products has two clear advantages over marketing them through traditional publishing houses:

- As info-product creator you keep 100 per cent of the profit compared with the percentage royalties you would obtain through traditional publishers – *if* they decide to publish your work at all.

- By retaining total control over the marketing of your product you can profit from it for as long as enough viable markets (willing, able, accessible buyers) exist.

Conversely, traditional publishers usually have so many new titles vying for their marketing budgets that unless an author is well-known, or the work is a bestseller, the writer's book is not given priority and usually ends up being pulled from the market within a year or two, plunging it into obscurity. That's the downside of being a traditionally published author: you must keep rolling out bestsellers if you are to earn ongoing residuals.

MARKETING OTHER PEOPLE'S PRODUCE

There is no shortage of opportunities to market info-product and software created by other online marketers and in subsequent chapters we will be highlighting a variety of leading sources. You won't make as much money of course (25 to 35 per cent commission as a general rule) but do bear in mind that this is passive income. You do something once, set the ball in motion, put your game plan on auto pilot, and keep on earning residuals for years after – providing of course that the product has an essential inbuilt longevity factor.

Benefits of reselling digital produce you don't create yourself include:

- No stockholding.
- No shipping charges.
- No depreciation.
- No debtors.
- No refunds.
- No breakages.

Don't go making choices yet. We still have a long way to go in our appreciation of what is entailed in selecting a profitable retirement pursuit.

5
Starting an offline business in retirement

It's a big decision to opt for an offline business as the route to a profitable retirement pursuit and it's one that you should not make rashly. For a start, would you be fit for it? It will take up a huge chunk of your time (perhaps take over your life for a while at the outset), cutting severely into other retirement interests. Would you have the finances for it? Might you find it stressful dealing face to face (perhaps for the first time in your life) with your prospective customers? Perhaps most importantly, are you willing to learn? (Incidentally, if you read my book *Your Retirement Masterplan* you may already be familiar with much of the substance of this chapter. That's okay; one more reading won't hurt. It will only serve to refresh your memory ...)

There are several crucial questions that need answers before pursuing the offline route.

HOW STRONG IS YOUR COMMITMENT?

Personal commitment is germane to success and it calls for certain disciplines. Now that you are retired you have time on your hands to pursue leisure interests that you only ever dreamed about when you were working; time to take a holiday whenever you want, to visit the grandchildren on the spur of the moment and much more besides.

- Do you really want to impinge on this free time by contracting to the full-time dedication that running an offline business will entail?

- Or is your disposition such that you could comfortably combine freedom and commitment?

WOULD YOU BE CAPABLE OF MAKING YOUR OWN DECISIONS?

You can listen to advice from other people of course but when it comes to making crucial commercial decisions affecting your own business, you will be out there on your own.

- Does the prospect faze you or are you capable of taking it all in your stride?

COULD YOU PLAN AHEAD TO COPE IN ALL KINDS OF WEATHER?

Success comes sooner when you develop the practice of creating individual strategies for every eventuality: good times, bad times, in-between times; rewarding and problematic situations.

- How do you rate yourself at planning ahead?
- Does it come easy to you or is it something you would need to work at?

DO YOU POSSESS GOOD INTERPERSONAL SKILLS?

You may be the most personable person you know, but how does your personality stack up in commercial terms? You will be dealing with a variety of people on a regular basis: staff, suppliers, customers, creditors, debtors, etc.

- Can you be objective yet affable in your dealings?
- Can you learn to put self interest on the back burner when required?

WOULD YOUR SPOUSE/PARTNER SUPPORT YOUR DECISION?

Having the unconditional support of your significant other is essential if you are to make a success of running an offline business in retirement.

• Will he/she feel left out, or play an active part in the endeavour?

• Will there be argument or agreement over finances?

On the other hand, if like me you are now alone in your third age journey you may quickly discover that entrepreneurship compensates in some small part for the loss of a partner.

CAN YOU AFFORD TO INVEST IN YOURSELF?

Perhaps for the first time ever you will be facing up to the prospect of investing not in tangibles such as a home or a motor car – but in yourself.

• Can you afford it at this time in your life?

• Even if you can comfortably afford it, do you really want to, even if the required investment is modest, or would you rather keep the money in the bank?

As with most things in life you have choices, but only you can decide what's best for *you*.

HOW ARE YOU AT HANDLING SETBACKS?

• What happens when you meet the odd inevitable setback?

• Will you wonder what on earth you've let yourself in for in what should be a less stressful time of your life?

• Conversely, do you possess the steeliness to convert apparent stumbling blocks into opportunities?

- Do you have the grit and enthusiasm to persevere and overcome in temporary adversity?

WHAT ABOUT THE FINANCIAL SIDE OF MATTERS?

If you were an employee during your working life, do you really have a thorough-enough understanding of the financial side of running your own business? To bring yourself up to speed, would you be prepared to take advantage of the abundance of free courses that exist on acquiring commercial nous?

ARE YOU READY TO CAPITALISE ON MAJOR CHANGE?

Your entry into the third age is a major change in its own right and for some, a culture shock.

- Are you ready to consider the implications of adding to your altered circumstances by starting a demanding offline business in retirement?

- Would taking this route cause you anxiety, or would you be confident about turning the transformation to your advantage?

DO YOU HAVE SPECIAL SKILLS?

Do you have special skills that would distinguish your business from the run of the mill? If so, consider yourself fortunate. Skills that are rare are always in demand and constitute the linchpin for a successful enterprise.

WHERE TO LOOK FOR HELP ON INITIAL PLANNING

Contact your local branch of a mainstream bank that specialises in small business development. Arrange an informal interview with the appropriate executive, outline your personal aims and give an indication of your current level of commercial expertise; then close this exploratory discussion by requesting their literature pack focusing on start-up support. Undertake this exercise *before* you settle on an idea for your retirement enterprise; it will give you a feel for what lies ahead should you decide to proceed.

Online alternative for sourcing assistance

If on the other hand you consider that it's too soon for a one-to-one dialogue, visit www.clearlybusiness.com (a Barclays Bank online initiative) where you will find reams of valuable free information on managing your accounts, controlling cash flow, raising start-up finance and much more besides. While you're there you can also order a copy of *Starting & Running Your Own Business* which will be delivered to your door in hard copy format within days. This comprehensive information wallet will provide you with a thorough grounding on the basics of planning an enterprise.

HOW TO FIND AND EVALUATE IDEAS

Start with yourself: where you are, where you've been, and where you'd like to be. Here are a few suggestions to get you started.

Could your leisure interests provide an opportunity?

We covered this earlier but let's look now at some hypothetical but practical possibilities.

- Perhaps you enjoy dressmaking and have a talent for design and the creation of exclusive patterns. Is there a market in your locality for producing made-to-measure garments for busy women who just don't have the time to shop?

- Does your hobby interest revolve around artificial floral/plant making and arranging? If so, you might consider cashing in on the growing trend of servicing local retail outlets; plants for the exterior, floral arrangements for indoors – and weddings.

- Do you have nimble fingers and a flair for macramé, mosaic art, or both? You can make key rings, belts, planters or wall hangings – and using tiny pieces of glass pebbles, tiles, or seeds you can create imaginative designs. These are ancient arts that are once again thriving. Could you supply local market traders? Ask around and show samples of your work.

- If your passion is for woodwork you might decide to specialise in a particular item or items of furniture or offer to build fittings to customers' own specifications.

Did you enjoy what you did when you were working full time?

Not everyone wants to return to the scene of the workplace but for some it provides the launch pad for a third age offline enterprise of their own creation. If you enjoyed what you did for a living you might derive some inspiration from these factual examples.

- Retired carpet fitters frequently set up in business to service retailers and consumers alike; the retailer saves on labour costs and the consumer on price.

- Service technicians in consumer electronics often create a steady retirement income stream by offering a maintenance/repairs service to both traders and the general public.

- Retired advertising executives set themselves up as catalysts for matching clients with agencies and/or introducing new business to ad agencies.

- Publishing employees can set up as a consultant advising would-be authors and/or offer a script reading service.

Look around and see how other retirees are doing it

Look around at what other retirees get up to in the way of operating part-time offline retirement businesses. You'll find that some of them are involved in callings like ...

- Answering service
- Antique dealership
- Bed and breakfast
- Building
- Catering
- Consulting service
- Day care
- Desktop publishing
- Florist
- Garage sales
- Garden maintenance
- Home handyman
- Image making
- Import/export
- Information broking
- Insurance broking
- Interior design
- Online auctions
- Painting and decorating
- Photography
- Plumbing
- Sundry online ventures

Several of the small businesses listed here make ideal third age offline ventures because they offer flexibility in terms of how much commitment you want to make, and for most of them you can use your own home as the base. Let's look at a few examples:

Bed & Breakfast

I have a friend in Colchester who runs a thriving B&B in retirement. He's now in his 70s and, like me, widowed. As he owns his property, goods and chattels, his running costs are minimal, and apart from food his only operating expense is the hire of a part-time cook cum server and housekeeper. His own involvement is marginal allowing him plenty of free time to pursue other retirement interests. Why did he choose to run a B&B? Because he had occasion to stay in many during his working life and reckoned he could do a better job than most of the establishments he visited.

Consulting Service

If you were fortunate enough in your career to acquire a skill or skills that are always in demand you would do well to consider setting up as a part-time consultant in retirement. Expertise is at a premium in all walks of industry and commerce, and isn't always available for full-time engagement. Start-up costs are minimal, operating expenses next to nothing, and you can commit to as much or as little time on the venture as you please. Calling on old contacts to begin with, you can gradually build up an income-generating clientele who will value the wisdom that accompanies greying hair.

Garden Maintenance

If you *really* enjoy looking after your own backyard, then garden maintenance is an ideal retirement venture. You can choose how many hours a week you want to work and you need virtually no capital outlay to start (you've probably already got most of the tools you'll need). And as more and more households now have both partners out working all day and continually stretched for leisure time, you won't have any problem finding customers. Add to that those people to whom gardening is an abomination: they all need your service. Moreover, if garden design and planning happens to be your *forté*, there are increasing numbers of new build homes that will welcome your expertise.

Home Handyman

If you were a tradesman or have always been a reliable DIY-er around the house, you could set yourself up to perform handyman services for those who can't do it themselves or don't have the time. Make it clear what you do and that you charge for your time. Save your customers money and build up a nice little income stream in your retirement years. If you already have the tools there is nothing to invest, and you can allocate your time flexibly. I have a brother-in-law (a retired colonel in the Royal Canadian Air Force) who runs his own home handyman business. He loves it – and reckons he's found his true calling at last!

HOW TO EVALUATE A SPECIFIC BUSINESS YOU HAVE IN MIND

Here are some questions to help clarify your thoughts:

- Is this something I will enjoy doing?
- My favourite activities are: ....
- I like to serve people by: ....
- Will it serve an expanding need for which there is no close substitute?
- Can I be so good at a specialised, targeted need that customers will think there is no close substitute?
- Can I handle the capital requirements?

- Can I learn the business by working for someone else first?

- Could I operate as a virtual operation, without a factory and with a minimum number of employees? (Virtual refers to a business where everything is outsourced, meaning you would subcontract manufacturing and packaging to outside sources.)

- Is this a product or service that I can test first?

- Should I consider a partner who has skills complementary to mine – or who could help finance the business?

HOW TO FINE TUNE THE SELECTION PROCESS

At the top of a blank sheet of paper, write the name of an activity you would like to pursue. (If there are several options and you haven't yet made up your mind, create a separate sheet for each alternative.) List as many businesses as you can come up with that are related to the activity, and then list all the relevant products or services. Use your imagination and jot down every conceivable contender. Refine the list to those businesses that do better in bad times (one may be appropriate for you). And now, for the purposes of illustration, let's focus on three examples from the list featured in 'Finding Ideas' (above): *Bed and Breakfast, Home Handyman, Garden Maintenance.* You can now make a comparative evaluation using the following hypothetical checklist (or better still your own checklist) with a 1–10 scoring system (10 being the highest):

Objective	Bed and Breakfast	Home Handyman	Garden Maintenance
Can I do what I love to do?	6	3	10
Will I fill an expanding need?	8	5	10
Can I specialise?	7	8	10
Can I learn it and test it first without committing to too much financial outlay?	9	8	9

This kind of analysis can help you gain objectivity in selecting your business.

Once you have decided what business you want to start ...

1. Construct your **for/against** list regarding characteristics of the business. On a blank piece of paper, draw a vertical line down the middle of the page and annotate on one side all the pros and on the other all the cons. Sometimes this will help to clarify your thinking.

2. Then write down the names of at least five successful businesses in your chosen field. Analyse what these concerns have in common and list the reasons that make them successful.

3. Talk to several people in your intended business. Don't be afraid of the negative aspects. Instead, seek out the pitfalls: better now than after you have committed yourself.

4. Write down the information you glean.

5. Observe the competition that are *not* doing well and analyse the reasons.

Making sure you become completely qualified

Before you even start to think about running an offline business, start thinking about how to become completely qualified:

*   The best way to become qualified is to go to work for someone in the same business – even if only for a few weeks.

*   Attend all classes you can on the subjects you need, for example: accounting, technology, selling.

*   Read all the appropriate how-to books you can locate.

*   Don't be afraid to ask questions or seek help from the most successful people in your intended business.

WHY YOU MUST TEST-MARKET WHEN YOU SETTLE ON AN IDEA

You now need to consider whether there is a quantifiable demand for your product or service – and the best way to establish that is to dip your toe in the water with some basic test-marketing. For example, you'd like to set up in business using your work skills to get two bites at the cherry like the retired carpet fitter and service technician. Here's what you do.

1. Create an outline for your idea.

2. Select your catchment area of operation, highlight the traders you'd like to service, make out lists of the residential areas where you reckon your direct customer base lives.

3. Bounce your idea off the local public sector small business advisory initiative (look them up in the telephone book or ask at the council offices). Armed with a well reasoned outline it should not prove difficult to persuade them to cover the costs of a modest-quantity two-colour flyer.

4. Produce your flyer, mail it to the traders, doorstep drop it in the residential areas.

5. Call on each trader individually and make a short presentation for your intended service.

6. Call on a small random sample of the accumulated residential areas to sniff out potential interest in your initiative.

If there is a product or produce involved in your initiative, do all of the foregoing but also spread some samples around and endeavour to gauge reaction. It's not rocket science but it's what you have to do to establish demand without incurring cost.

HOW RESEARCH IRONS OUT THE WRINKLES

Even if the results of your test-marketing fill you with confidence, it is good practice to undertake some additional research to ascertain whether there are still a few wrinkles lurking around that need to be ironed out. There are several ways you might do this, but here is one that worked for me and it cost me nothing. I visited the best search engine of them all www.google.com to find out everything I could about the feasibility of my idea. I did this before I launched my part-time self publishing venture (on which more at the end of this chapter) and located six superb articles which saved me needless anguish later on. In one of these I discovered that I could do most of the work on my domestic computer, thus necessitating only minimal outsourcing. This particular article also knocked back some other ham-fisted notions I'd been harbouring about getting the business up and running in other directions. All of this I could equally have gleaned by talking with a start-up consultant, but doing it that way would have set me back several hundred pounds.

THE NUTS AND BOLTS OF RUNNING AN OFFLINE BUSINESS

Your route map is starting to take shape and this is where the hard work begins. You should now be thinking in terms of getting to the heart of running your own offline business by engaging in further research and development before you arrange follow-up meetings with the bank and the small business advisory initiative. Next you ought to be making provision for appointing an accountant and solicitor (if required). The closer you get to what will make your enterprise tick, the more readily you will be able to access assistance from the professionals. There is much still to be done but lots of assistance is available to help you get there and towards the end of this section I will direct you to:

1   An online source offering free tuition on most of the essential aspects.

2   A public sector offline source that may cost you a little, but is worth the investment.

Let's start with a suggestion for the template of your all-important business plan.

HOW TO CREATE YOUR BUSINESS PLAN

Not everyone likes writing reports and that basically is what your business plan will be: a report. It will be the instrument that not only keeps you focused on your goals, but the means to attracting any external investment you may require. Borrow a book on the subject from your local public lending library and learn from an expert. Meantime, here are some of the basic elements you will want to include:

- Explain exactly how your business idea works in practice.
- Describe your objectives.
- Define the marketplace.
- Research the competition.
- Produce a clear account of your product or service.
- Explain the key aspects of your sales policy.
- Develop a strategy to market the enterprise.
- Crystallise the strengths and weaknesses of your idea.
- Make out a case for financial assistance.
- Show how you will fund the business.
- Describe the market, its characteristics and current trends.
- Show precisely where your product or service fits in.

Now summarise the overall content and position it accordingly.

DECIDING YOUR BUSINESS STATUS

You have a choice of routes and the eventual decision will largely depend on the nature of your offline retirement business.

Becoming a sole trader

If you are planning to work on your own, your best bet is to become a sole trader. It's the simplest way to own a business and will keep your legal costs to a minimum. You'll need to tell the Inland Revenue of your initiative (unless it's non-revenue producing) but as a sole trader, all the profits from the business will be yours. On the downside, any debt you take on board will also be your responsibility.

Forming a partnership

If you intend to invite other people to become involved as principals, you might want to consider setting up as a partnership. This is similar to operating as a sole trader except that all of the costs and profits are shared between the partners. A partnership can also allow the responsibility and work to be equally shared, which can lessen the pressure on you. Whatever you decide, draw up a partnership agreement to protect your own interests bearing in mind that all debt incurred is an individual *and* collective liability.

Partnership agreements should always include provision for:

- Partnership shares;
- Partnership property;
- Capital;
- Drawings;
- Accounts;
- Restrictions to protect other partners;
- Comprehensive termination provisions to protect ongoing partners.

Forming a limited company

This is a more complicated form of business ownership. As a director of a limited company you will not be personally responsible for the debts of your business as a company is separate from its owners. You will pay yourself a salary just like any other employee. However, running a limited company entails very specific rules and regulations, and will require the assistance of a solicitor and accountant. Initial set-up costs will be higher as you will need to register with Companies House and submit regular financial statements.

WHAT TO CONSIDER WHEN CHOOSING A TRADING NAME

This is a crucial exercise you will need to address as soon as possible. It can make or break any business, offline or online. List as many ideas as you can before deciding on the name your enterprise is to trade under. Getting it right from the start is essential – you don't want to have to change it after a few months. The secret is to adopt the KISS approach (Keep it Simple Stupid) and there are a few house rules to become familiar with before proceeding further. In essence, the ideal trading name should meet these five requirements:

1. No more than seven letters in the composition of the core word in the title, preferably five.

2. No more than three syllables in the pronunciation of the core word, preferably two.

3. The name must look and sound right.

4. It must fit the purpose of the enterprise.

5. It must be legally acceptable.

Using your own name is quite alright and it makes sense if you are setting up as a consultant of one type or another. But keep it simple. Not 'Humphrey D. Lestocque Insurance Services', but rather 'Lestocque Insurance', for example, using the core words to best effect. There is a lot in a name: get it right from the outset.

FINANCING AN OFFLINE BUSINESS

You need to give early attention as to how much money is required to get started. In fact you'll need to consider very carefully whether you want to enter into any business that entails considerable financial outlay at a time in your life when it might be unwise to embrace that sort of commitment. This could discolour your entire business plan and if it will cause you to worry, don't do it. Conversely, if you are converting a lifetime hobby into a business, your investment will probably be very small.

Possible sources of finance include:

1. Personal savings.

2. Insurance policies.

3. Annuities.

4. Spare equity in your home.

5. Friends and relations.

6. Bank loan.

7. Public sector assistance.

It is highly unlikely that your bank manager will demonstrate much enthusiasm about handing over hard cash on the strength of a business proposal from a retiree without the evidence of other funding in position. Your first port of call then should be to the neighbourhood offices of NewDeal 50Plus*. Listen to what they have to say and if they offer you assistance in any shape or form, take it. Next, pay a visit to the local council business development unit where (assuming your plan is sound and the proposition viable) you may gain access to grants and/or soft loans that are not normally available. Now you can go your bank manager …

WHY FINDING THE RIGHT LOCATION IS VITAL

Where you locate will depend on the nature of your retirement business and you must give consideration to premises as you are putting together your business plan and initial budget. If you are to be a retailer you will need a shop, or a factory if you are to be

* see www.newdeal.gov.uk/newdeal.asp?DealId=50PLU

manufacturing something or other: for both of these examples go first to the public sector where you might be offered what you need at a peppercorn rent. Try though to locate at home and for most third age commercial initiatives that is a distinct possibility; it conserves cash and is quite acceptable nowadays to most funding sources. If you need a separate telephone line or a 'front office' make appropriate provision in your budgeting.

GETTING ORGANISED AT THE OUTSET

Will you be going it alone or will you need staff? Only you and your business idea will determine that. If you need assistance go first once again to the public sector. They will identify trained personnel (or cover training costs) and provide employment grants where appropriate.

ALLOWING FOR ACCOUNTING AND CASH FLOW

Do you have basic book-keeping/accounting skills? If not, consider attending an evening class. Even if you are going to use an accountant, you still need to know the rudiments so as to be able to exercise financial control over your business and manage the cash flow efficiently. An online alternative you might want to consider is Dave Marshall's website www.coursepal.com. Dave is a management accountant by profession and offers comprehensive free instruction for beginners. You can either participate in his tutorial online or download the e-book version to study offline at your own convenience.

ALLOWING FOR TAXATION

Not a subject we need delve into in detail this early in your potential adventure, but it would be prudent to make some allowance for it.

You should be thinking in terms of:

1. Income tax;

2. National Insurance contributions (NIC);

3. Value Added Tax (VAT).

Preparing your accounts

Should your business turnover (total sales) before expenses fall below £15,000 for a full year of trading, you will not be required to provide detailed accounts. Instead, a simple three-line summary will suffice. For example:

Turnover	£14,657
Less purchases & expenses	£ 5,500
Net profits	**£ 9,157**

COMPUTER AND COMMUNICATION SKILLS

If you are currently short on either or both of these vital skills you will need to get up to speed as quickly as possible to make the most of your enterprise. Further on in this section you will find online and offline avenues of valuable instruction. Choose one and apply yourself before you launch your business – even if you are just doing it for pleasure.

LEARNING HOW TO MARKET THE ENTERPRISE

There is no mystique about marketing. It is all down to commonsense and practical application. Ignore the hype and concentrate on the essentials.

1. Costing.

2. Price setting.

3. Buying.

4. Merchandising.

5. Selling.

and only if you really need them ...

6. Advertising.

7. Public relations.

8. Exhibitions.

Once again you will find ample practical instruction online or offline as featured below.

ACQUIRING COMMERCIAL SKILLS ONLINE

Back to online learning: go to this ultra-professional non-profit website www.myownbusiness.org where you can access *completely free of charge* an MBA-calibre online course on how to go about setting up a business in retirement. It comes complete with 12 wide-ranging lessons and 33 powerful sound bites (in a variety of digital formats) from successful entrepreneurs, plus interactive feedback for each session. You get all of this without having to invest a penny. It covers in depth all of the elements we've just touched on and even if you are not on the internet at home you can still access this comprehensive course for free at your local library. As it does not require online participation you may download/print out the entire programme to study at home in your own time.

ADDING TO YOUR SKILLS OFFLINE

Online learning is extremely useful for getting up to speed on theory, but if you are *really* serious about pursuing this retirement option I suggest you put yourself down for one of the many business start-up programmes sponsored by the Department for Work and Pensions. Don't be put off by the maximum age cut off point. If you are sufficiently persuasive you will gain admittance. I did, and I did so because no matter how much you *think* you know about commerce, you can never learn enough, let alone too much.

Here is an example of a typical syllabus:

- New business planning.
- Markets and market selection.
- Product identification.
- Marketing.
- Computer training.
- Support systems for start-ups.
- Financial planning.
- Public sector funding.
- Private sector funding.
- Sourcing proven ideas.
- Legal aspects.

It may cost you a little to participate but it will be money well spent if your heart is set on starting a business in retirement whether for fun or profit.

CRUCIAL QUESTIONS TO ASK YOUR PROFESSIONAL ADVISERS

Armed with all of this intelligence you will be more than able to field questions from your professional advisers – but here are some crucial questions you might want to ask them ...

Your solicitor

1. What are my legal obligations if I opt for sole trader status?
2. Explain to me the significance of individual and collective responsibility for debts incurred in a partnership arrangement?

3. How much will it cost me to set up a limited company?

4. Will I need more than one director?

5. Must I produce an annual return even though my turnover is small?

Your accountant

1. Which accounting books should I keep?

2. Are there different accounting procedures according to business status: sole trader, partnership, limited company?

3. What records should I maintain for taxation purposes?

4. How much do I have to be turning over before I register for VAT?

5. How much will you charge me for the annual audit (for a limited company)?

Your bank manager

1. Can you provide me with an overdraft facility?

2. If not, what are your best terms for a small business loan?

3. What are your charges for administering a small business current account?

4. If I get lucky and want to place money on deposit, what's the best rate of interest you can offer me?

5. How often do you need to see management accounts: monthly, quarterly, half-yearly?

Your public sector funding contact

1. Would I qualify for small business grant?

2. Could you offer me a 'soft' loan facility?

3. Tell me about employment grants and how they operate.

4. What are your terms for office/small factory rental accommodation?

5. Could I obtain a training grant?

6. What else can you offer me?

CAUTIONARY NOTE

If you think I'm deliberately putting obstacles in your way to dissuade you from starting up in an offline business then you will be wrong. I operate one myself in retirement and derive tremendous satisfaction from it. What this chapter has set out to accomplish is to caution you that the commitment factor in offline trading is considerably higher than that relating to online enterprise.

Let me put that another way.

You can close down an online business at no cost with just a click of your mouse button but winding up an offline business that isn't fulfilling your ambitions is both difficult and expensive.

Bear in mind too that going offline for your profitable retirement pursuit means you will be foregoing the opportunity to create streams of residual income – the subject matter of much of the remainder of this book.

6

Why online is faster, easier and less stressful

When you adopt the online route to pursue profitable activity in retirement you eliminate the bulk of the hassles connected with setting up an offline business. Even so, you will still need to embark on a prescribed learning curve (and that's what the next 27 chapters are all about) but it's a lot more fun. All things considered, online is the faster, easier, less stressful route to take for retirees who wish to add to their basic income. Your virtual store can be any size you like – as big as the biggest mall in New York City – and there is no limit on the amount of products you can offer: the range can be infinite.

And how's this for a list of inbuilt advantages when you deal in digitised produce?

1. Minimal start-up costs.
2. Work your own hours.
3. 24-hour trading.
4. Open 365 days a year.
5. Marketplace: the planet Earth.
6. Level playing field even if your website consists of a solitary page.
7. Automatic order taking.
8. Automatic payment processing.
9. Instant delivery of produce.
10. Instant shopper satisfaction.

11. No customer interfacing.

12. No premises.

13. No rent.

14. No commercial rates.

15. No staff.

16. No wages.

17. No stock.

18. No creditors.

19. No debtors.

20. No shipping.

21. Opportunity to create passive income online.

We haven't even scratched the surface, but don't you already get the feeling that the online route sounds faster, easier and less stressful?

TRIM START-UP COSTS TO THE BARE MINIMUM

You can start an online retirement business for next to nothing when you trade in digitised merchandise. Apart from your domain name (and this comes dirt cheap nowadays) your only other basic start-up costs comprise page creation tools and website hosting, but I'll show you in Chapter 16 how to obtain all three in a unique piece of software that offers a great deal more besides. I'll also direct you in Chapter 23 to another software tool that will produce your initial e-produce for free.

SET WORKING HOURS TO SUIT YOUR NEW LIFESTYLE

For many retirees this is the single most attractive aspect of running an internet business. If you feel like working 10 hours on a given day you can do so; if you feel less energetic, then you set the schedule to suit yourself; one hour, two or three – or take the day off and apply yourself to other interests. There is no requirement for you to be strapped to your computer because, as you will discover as you progress in your studies, almost *everything* connected with the enterprise can be set to automatic pilot.

HOW YOUR WEBSITE CAN TAKE ORDERS WHILE YOU SLEEP

The automation I just referred to can be positioned to accept orders electronically every second of every day and every night. We'll examine your options in Chapter 30 where I will also let you in on my favourite order-taking software; how it works; how inexpensive it is to operate – and why it is the perfect solution for the small online business dealing exclusively in digitised produce.

WHY THERE'S 365 DAY NON-STOP TRADING IN CYBERSPACE

It can't help it. The internet is always open; it doesn't even close down for a quick breather. It ignores public holidays and it never takes a vacation.

- Can you imagine the scope this unique marketing opportunity presents in your pursuit of a profitable retirement?

- Can you envisage how vast the cyberspace marketplace will become when within the next few years the 55 million existing customer base will be extended by many millions more as Asian users kick in?

- Can you think of any offline business that is faster, easier and less stressful?

- Can you see now why so many of today's retirees are turning to the internet as the route to take to add to basic income?

It gets even better when you learn how to combine both online and offline in promoting your ideas. I'll show you how I do it in a later chapter.

HOW YOUR LOCAL STORE DOES BUSINESS INTERNATIONALLY

The local store housed in your computer is contained in a microchip measuring less than half the size of a postage stamp and yet it has the power to reach across the globe and do business internationally. You can't see how this would be of much use to you? Then allow me to illustrate from my own experience. Eighteen months ago I launched an information product that was intended for local writing groups. What do I find a year and a half on? 92 per cent of downloads are from the USA, seven per cent from the European Union, and only one per cent from the UK. There's a logical reason for this which we'll discuss in some detail in the penultimate chapter.

HOW YOU'LL COMPETE WITH THE MOGULS ON EQUAL TERMS

Providing the virtual stall you set up is of the highest standards (and there is no problem in attaining these) then you will be competing on equal terms with the major dot coms. You could be operating your little empire from a desk in your living room overlooking the village green, but no one will ever know. That's the beauty of online trading: *anonymity*. It provides a level playing field for everyone and no one can steal a march on you because by the time you have finished reading this book you will know how to access the same marketing tools the moguls use – and they will work for you even if your site consists of a solitary sales page.

WHY AUTOMATIC ORDERING EASES THE STRAIN

When people visit your website and review your digitised information produce or software they make one of four decisions:

1. They buy on the spot.

2. They decide to move on and find something better, cheaper – or for free.

3. They decide to come back again later for a second look.

4. They decide they're not interested.

When they decide to buy on the spot (or return later to buy) they want the merchandise immediately and they want it without any hassle. With automatic ordering they can have what they want because the entire transaction takes only seconds.

$$ORDER \rightarrow PROCESS \rightarrow DELIVERY$$

WHY AUTOMATIC PROCESSING GETS THE CASH IN FAST

Virtual transactions get the cash in fast because the process is fully automatic:

- Customer produces credit card details online.

- Transaction is authorised.

- Sale receipts are deposited in your virtual account.

You will need a facility to accept credit cards because without one you will miss out on 90 per cent of the potential sales for your e-produce. I will give the two best options in Chapter 30.

HOW DELIVERING PRODUCE INSTANTLY CREATES GOODWILL

Online it's win-win all round. The customer gets the produce, you get the cash, and you both get what you want instantly. A bond is created and in retail parlance that equals goodwill. How you use it is your business, but you would do well to nurture its power.

WHY CUSTOMER SATISFACTION MEANS MORE SALES

The most productive avenue for future sales will always remain the list of customers who previously bought from you and were happy with the purchase. The potential here for additional sales far outstrips any strategy you might put in place to attract new business.

WHY VIRTUAL CUSTOMER INTERFACING REDUCES STRESS

In an offline business, customer interfacing can prove arduous. It is ongoing and covers issues such as product information, demonstration, general enquiries, and complaints. Virtual interfacing eliminates the stress. Answers or directions covering most customer issues can be hosted in a web page devoted to **Frequently Asked Questions** (FAQ).

SIX WAYS YOU'LL SAVE ON OPERATING COSTS

1. You don't need premises therefore you pay neither rent nor commercial rates.

2. You don't need staff therefore you won't have a wages bill.

3. You don't have to carry stock therefore you won't incur depreciation costs.

4. You won't have creditors therefore you save on accounting costs.

5. You won't have debtors therefore you don't have to fund transactions.

6. You won't be shipping produce therefore you won't have freight charges.

CREATING PASSIVE INCOME ONLINE

When you go online for your profitable retirement pursuit you also open the door to creating passive income as we shall discover in the next chapter.

7

How to create passive income in cyberspace

The formula you would use to create passive income in cyberspace is an extension of the one described in Chapter 4 and it works this way: you identify residual income streams, generate appropriate e-produce, and put the whole thing on remote control using the automatic processes we've just touched on. This is the formula that all top notch online marketers use and it is equally available for you to employ in your own profitable retirement pursuit. Let me give you a working example. I have a little website I built years ago and to which I only refer occasionally to check on returns. Whenever I do, I find that it's still clocking up two or three downloads per month without any input from me. It may not add up to much but it's all grist to the mill.

BECOME A MASTER OF THE UNEXPECTED

You can use the unexpected to good effect in creating passive income to bolster your pension and savings in retirement. Ideas that are offbeat and at odds with the norm are often the very ones that stimulate interest and produce results. We reviewed six such ideas in Chapter 3 and towards the end of this section I'll give you two more that work as online income generators for many pro-active retirees.

First though let me tell you a story …

WHAT WAS SANTA DOING IN A BOAT?

More years ago than I care to remember, I had occasion to dabble in the unexpected with spectacular results. At the time I was assistant publicity manager of a large department store and still wet behind the ears in matters of marketing. As a test, my immediate superior charged me with responsibility of handling a major annual promotional event: the arrival of Father Christmas at his in-store grotto. Traditionally the fat merry old gentleman made his appearance at the main entrance in a makeshift sleigh, a journey of some 50 yards from the company garage nearby. This year the management wanted something different and my first thought was to have Santa descend on the roof in a helicopter, but the local constabulary soon put the kibosh on that. Then the office junior came up with the idea of ferrying St Nick up the river in a pleasure steamer, disembarking at the main city quay, close to the store. As it happens the lad's dad was the harbourmaster and he reckoned that all permissions would be readily forthcoming. I then set about convincing my boss about the merits of the scheme. He grudgingly conceded that the incongruity of the scenario might just reap dividends. On the other hand if it failed I'd be the one to walk the plank. The local media were appraised of the initiative and notices were fly-posted at city centre vantage points. They looked like this.

WHAT IS SANTA

DOING IN A BOAT?

Join the crowds and

see for yourself at

Riverside Quay

SATURDAY 9.30am

The day arrived and so did a crowd numbering in excess of 3,000 screaming kids accompanied by their embarrassed parents. They were not alone. The local news media turned out in force together with a crew from the BBC television programme *Children's Roundabout*. In those days the BBC had no competition on the airwaves and so this resulted in blanket nationwide coverage, and the clip proved so popular that it became the opening sequence of the programme for many months to follow. The store management were delighted with the free exposure and even more delighted with the record Christmas toy sales that ensued.

Why am I telling you all this?

Simply to illustrate the power of the unexpected when you bend the rules to create interest – exactly what transforms the following two ideas into passive income generators.

GIVE IT ALL AWAY FOR FREE

Imagine a multi-page website where everything on show is for free. There are dozens of worthwhile offers but your visitors cannot buy any of them. Anything that takes their fancy they simply procure at no charge; not just downloadable produce but tangible merchandise that they requisition online. You think that's crazy? Read on.

SIMULATE THE POSTAL BARGAINS TECHNIQUE

Imagine a similar website where the pages are divided into identically squared off boxes (much like the postal bargain ads in yesteryear's newspapers). On this occasion your visitors have to pay for the merchandise – but at up to half regular store prices.

QUESTIONS ARISING

- Where can you find stuff to give away for free?
- How do you make a profit?
- Where can you find stuff to sell at half the normal price?

HOW IT WORKS

The stuff you give away for free comes from speciality test-marketing operations that pay you a commission every time someone downloads a freebie from your website or responds to the link in your promotional emails. The stuff you sell at half the regular price comes from dropshipping warehouses on a similar commission per sale basis.

WHERE YOU FIND SOURCES OF SUPPLY

You find them on the same medium you use to market the produce: *online*. Try Google using appropriate keywords such as 'free merchandise suppliers' and 'cut price merchandise suppliers'. You will be presented with lots of alternatives. Choose those with the merchandise you would feel most comfortable marketing.

WHAT'S IN IT FOR YOU?

You sit at home at your computer controlling a worldwide emporium; you have no investment and no stock to purchase or warehouse; your website visitor orders are fulfilled automatically online; your sales/commissions are electronically processed and the cash banked in your account automatically. What you won't do is make a fortune because this is passive drip feed marketing which takes time (but little effort) to build. Think about this though: your store is open 24/7 and your market is almost infinite.

Added bonus

Every time someone makes contact they leave behind their email address which you can use for future approaches.

WHAT'S REQUIRED OF YOU?

You will need some basic web page building skills to take advantage of the illustrated avenues of the unexpected but that's not a problem because everything you need to know is right here in this book. When you're up to speed, put your own mind to work and you will uncover other twists of the unexpected to convert into passive retirement income generators.

There are many other ways to locate potential product and service ideas that may prove suitable as passive income generators and I'll now list some of these.

JOIN AN ONLINE FORUM OR DISCUSSION GROUP

I guarantee that if you see the same questions repeated in a forum or discussion group, there are hundreds, possibly thousands, of other people out there wondering *exactly* the same thing.

Here's why: only a small percentage of the online community participates in forums and discussion groups. So, if the question is popular among these people, you can be sure that there are many others surfing the web, searching for the equivalent.

Some good places to start looking for discussion boards and newsgroups related to your area of interest include …

www.groups.google.com
www.talkcity.com
www.insidetheweb.com
www.forumone.com

CHECK OUT CONSUMER REVIEW WEBSITES

Check out consumer review websites to find out what people like and dislike about branded e-produce. Surfers use these sites to rave or complain, and that makes them great places to learn exactly what the public thinks about your competitors – or perhaps even you sometime in the future …

Some good sites to examine include:

www.consumerreview.com
www.consumersearch.com
www.consumersdigest.com

… but a quick search in any major search engine should also produce good boards and chat rooms to check out.

JOIN AN AFFILIATE PROGRAMME

Affiliate Programmes are also referred to as Associate or Reseller, Commission or Pay-Per-Sale, Pay-Per-Click and Click-Through. Joining an affiliate programme is a useful way to start earning passive income indirectly on the internet (should you decide that creating your own produce is not for you). All you do is to refer someone else's product or service for which you receive a referral fee for every confirmed sale. How it works: you are assigned a special URL that tracks all of the visitors you send to the principal's website – and more significantly, also tracks the sales that you generate.

It's extremely easy to put into practice. You just post a link, a banner, or a short recommendation letter on your website, or perhaps recommend the product or service in your newsletter or ezine, and then collect a percentage of the profits when a sale is made.

You don't ever worry about …

- creating the product;
- packaging;
- shipping;
- collecting the money;
- customer service.

The system is simple to set up and there is really very little work involved. Once the link is there you are guaranteeing yourself an extremely easy source of income for years to come (*passive income*). These earn-per-sale programmes are usually really easy to join but make sure you read the terms and conditions because they can vary from one opportunity to another.

I should also mention that there are a number of associate pay-per-lead or per-click opportunities. In pay-per-lead you are paid every time your customer fills out a survey, asks for more information, or gets a quote on a product (in other words, you are paid for giving the company a contact). You may even get paid every time your customer downloads trial or demo software.

Pay-per-click is very similar. Basically, you get paid every time someone clicks through the link from your site to the owner's website (whether a text link or graphic link).

Make sure that you do business with reputable companies

Some affiliate operators work really hard, make a lot of sales for the companies they represent, and are forced to wait months on end for their commission (some *never* get paid at all for the sales they generate). Such irresponsible principals do not take their affiliates seriously, aren't using the proper software, and are wasting time and money doing tedious chores by hand when they should be fully automated. So while there are some really fantastic opportunities around that can earn you a sizeable income, you do need to do your homework in advance of commitment.

Two really good sites to visit to find high quality associate opportunities that pay excellent referral fees:

www.associateprograms.com
www.refer-it.com/

Fig. 2. Industry newsletter and affiliate notification service.

Deal only with the associate programmes these two sites rate highly and avoid the heartache and frustration of the fraudsters out there peddling get-rich-quick rip-offs. Chapter 12 contains an in-depth review on the subject of affiliate reselling as a candidate for passive income generation in retirement.

DO AN EMAIL SURVEY USING YOUR OWN CUSTOMER BASE

Surveys are not only a great way to discover how to make improvements to existing products or services they also excel at unearthing fresh ideas. You won't be able to take advantage of this option straightaway but you will in time when you've built your initial customer base.

Once you've sold something to someone once it becomes easier *to sell to them over and over again.*

In fact, research statistics indicate that your client base is a gold mine and that *as many as 36 per cent of people who have bought something from you previously will buy again* if you have something similar to offer. Consider the potential here and take advantage of this highly profitable relationship. Find out what your previous customers are asking for with an email survey.

Think about it – an email survey isn't going to cost you anything but time.

8

Twenty ways to use your computer to make money

In Chapter 3 we reviewed an 'idea format' for improving aspects of a product or service created by someone else. Now is your opportunity to put it to the test. If you cannot come up with an idea of your own or you are still unsure about affiliate reselling, here are 20 alternative opportunities worthy of your consideration. Whatever level of internet expertise you currently possess, there's a profitable online retirement pursuit for you in this extensive selection. Among the examples are openings for the highly skilled, the semi-skilled, the totally unskilled – and with appropriate planning, you could run several of these ventures concurrently. They're as new as the internet itself and they are already being successfully worked by retiree home-based operators like yourself.

Several of the descriptions to follow contain URLs that will take you to websites where you can learn more – or see for yourself how someone else is marketing the opportunity. For those options that take your fancy, but for which you are short on skills, there is ample training available online and usually for free. How much income you can expect to earn is down to the quality of your planning, your willingness to learn, and your application. What's more, almost all of them have the potential for passive income generation.

1 – MAKE MONEY FROM OTHER PEOPLE'S KNOW-HOW

Several years ago a lady from the United States came up with a very simple but powerful plan for making money on the internet: a method that anyone can copy and profit from.

Here is what she did:

On AOL there is a forum called 'Business Know-How'. Within this forum there is a section 'File Libraries'. The file libraries contain articles that people have uploaded (posted) to the forum. These people may be marketing consultants, software publishers, book publishers or writers and other experts. They post the articles in order to get exposure to internet users who may be interested in their services. By looking at the download statistics for the articles, the lady in question was able to determine which reports were the most popular with members of the forum.

As a matter of fact, the number of times a file has been downloaded is invariably posted right on the main screen and since you can sort the articles by number of downloads, it is an easy task to find the most popular titles. Now these articles are usually only 3 or 4 pages long but they contain a wealth of information on just about everything to do with operating a business including advertising, management, pricing, start-ups, business plans, organisation, marketing, etc.

She downloaded several of the most promising articles and wrote to the authors to ask for two things:

1. Permission to reprint the reports on CD.
2. Permission to transfer the reprint rights to others.

Now, why on earth would these authors give her permission to reprint their copyrighted material? For the same reason they had uploaded the articles in the first place: free publicity. They know that the more people who view their articles, the more exposure they will get for their products and services – and the better chance they have of making a sale. For them, it's free advertising – and for her, it represents a never-ending source of fresh, new reports.

After she got permission from the authors to reprint their articles, she grouped them together according to subject matter and produced 12

CDs that featured a different business topic. Each disk contained five to eight different reports relating to the topic. At the bottom of each report there is a 'plug' for the author. This plug is sometimes called a resource box and generally contains the author's name, contact reference, and information about the product or service on offer. It looks just like a classified ad.

Now (bearing in mind that the lady is selling reports, not the product or service) this is where she got really smart. Instead of just selling the CDs individually herself, she came up with the idea of an opportunity catalogue and offered the disks for sale in four different ways:

- **Retail** – You could buy each disk for $8.

- **Reprint** – You could buy the reprint rights to a disk for between $100 and $150 and sell the disk to others at retail.

- **Unlimited** – You could buy the reprint rights to a disk and also the right to sell the reprint rights to others. This option cost $180 to $250 depending on the disk. Or, if you were really serious about making money, you could buy the …

- **Business in a Box** – You could buy unlimited reprint and resell rights to all the disks for $2000. Many people went for the Business in a Box option because she included a discount coupon for $1000 if they ordered within a certain date that was stamped in red on the coupon.

The last I heard, she had sold 100 Business in a Box packages for $1000 each in less than a year. **Total turnover: $100,000.**

Anyone could do what this lady did because there are literally hundreds of thousands of valuable, informative free reports and dissertations (including hundreds of my own) on the internet – and all of these are there just waiting to be downloaded and marketed successfully. These reports are not just restricted to business services; you will unearth a cache of downloadable documents covering every topic from health care to dog grooming, from A to Z.

At first glance this might appear like a convoluted way to do business, but in reality it is very simple – and it's a proven winner – and makes for an ideal profitable retirement pursuit. There are unlimited numbers of authoritative, well written, free reports available for download on the internet, reports from authors who are only too willing to let you have them to do with what you please – providing always you obtain resale permission rights where required.

The lady sourced her articles from the AOL forum but here is a list of 11 other websites containing similar (if not better) material:

ezinearticles.com
www.certificate.net/wwio
www.ideamarketers.com
www.marketing-seek.com
www.goarticles.com
www.netterweb.com
www.articlesfactory.com
www.worldabooks.com/writers-connection/
www.web-source.net/syndicator_submit.htm
www.searchwarp.com
www.addme.com

Give serious consideration to this first option for a profitable retirement pursuit because if handled professionally it could prove a real money-spinner. In the Appendix you'll find an even bigger list of sources containing many more sites where you can download valuable articles for free with permission in most cases to do what you like with them.

2 – RUN YOUR OWN CYERSPACE AD AGENCY

If you are sufficiently motivated to become competent in using and explaining the workings of the internet to small businesses in your locality, you could build up a home based Internet Ad Agency serving clients in a specialised area. The best way to start is to focus on a market with which you are familiar. You could for example set up a website to attract advertising from the travel and tourism industry or you could specialise in one type of service. For example, a website devoted to wedding planning will attract advertising revenue from local hotels, restaurants, florists, car hire, bakeries, etc.

How you make money

You can lease a virtual server that will hold 5000 pages (or more) for around £75 per month. If you offer your clients designed/maintained web pages at £10 per page, you will only need to sell eight pages to meet the expense. The goal must be to get as many clients as you can, thus maximising the profitability of your server capacity.

You can also offer custom design services on an hourly basis. Charge between £55 and £80 per hour – or determine your rates on a per-job basis, taking into account all billable hours involved in the project. Many internet ad agencies also work on monthly retainers of £250 or more, providing updating and maintenance. An example of this might be updating the menu on a restaurant web page.

In essence, your incomings derive from:

- advertising revenue;
- mix of hosting/design/maintenance fees.

Getting started

You'll need to set up some sample ads on your domain to show to potential clients.

Into the future

This is a business with enormous growth potential where you can develop a close relationship with your clientele. You'll be servicing an area you know about and enjoy – but remember that (as a one-person agency) you must be hands-on in every aspect of the process; from selling ads to designing and maintaining the web pages.

Maybe you owned (as I did), worked in or managed a traditional advertising agency during your 'active' years. Here's an opportunity to do it all over again from home as a retiree cyberspace specialist.

3 – BECOME A CLIP ART SPECIALIST

Clip arts are those ready-to-use illustrations, borders, stylised headlines, and other little pieces of art that you add to brighten up ads, leaflets, newsletters, etc. Before the emergence of new age electronic technology, the main sources for clip art were office supply stores and mail order dealers – but now you can find a sizeable quantity on your computer – and an even bigger selection from the internet. And all for free. Moreover, there are many software packages now available as free downloads that will permit you to create your own copyright-free graphics which you can sell on to other users. The clip art business isn't everyone's cup of tea but if there's a creative streak in you bursting to break out, you might do very well in this home-based opportunity to make money online.

4 – OFFER A HOME-BASED DESKTOP PUBLISHING SERVICE

According to research findings, this market had expanded globally from £1.8 million in annual sales in 1985 to almost £4.1 *billion* in 2004 – and there would appear to no end in sight to its phenomenal growth. One of the very real challenges of this business is that there are millions of potential clients out there who are still unaware that they need the services of a desktop specialist. Home-based desktop publishers are engaged in producing a welter of graphic materials: brochures, flyers, advertisements, newsletters, books, business proposals and forms. Some also provide word processing services for their clients while others will work on almost any type of graphic assignment. This is an enormous market where the proficient operator can locate endless opportunities for residual income. It's a superb business for retirees who have the technical know-how, enthusiasm, and the will to succeed.

5 – CREATE, REGISTER, AUCTION OFF DOMAIN NAMES

Several years ago the UK national daily press carried a story about an enterprising young man who exercised considerable foresight when he registered the domain name www.bettingshop.com. Why? Because a few months later he sold it in an internet auction for £25,000! The trick is to locate and register domain names that sometime or another certain big businesses and/or institutions will pay handsomely to have the rights transferred. There's a website where you can do an instant free search on any number of names you can think up and then proceed to register as many domains as you wish at under £10 a throw. Why not get your thinking cap on? Come up with some likely candidates, visit this website www.whois.com and start registering. Who knows, there might be £25,000 – and a profitable retirement pursuit for you. And here's another website worth investigating: www.OpenForSale.com.

Fig. 3. Learn how to find buyers for your domain names.

It features a weekend crash course with 25 breakthrough strategies to help you automatically find buyers for your names. This imaginative tutorial costs $37 (approx. £20) but it could pay for itself several times over within days of applying its well reasoned directives.

In Chapter 11 you will discover how to use eBay for auctioning off your selected domain names.

6 – PROVIDE A PRODUCT ENDORSEMENT SERVICE

Do you miss out because you don't have a product or service of your own? Not necessarily. There are numerous traders who would love to give you a piece of the action if you agree to promote their merchandise to readers of your ezine (newsletter). In general terms, you split the proceeds 50/50 with the product owner.

Product endorsement works best when:

- You work with traders who have products that closely match the interests of your readership. If you publish an ezine relating to the grooming of dogs, a good product would be a book/CD/DVD on dog training – and better still, something entitled 'Dog Grooming Secrets of the Professionals'. Sticking in something like 'How to Bathe Your Cat' would clearly be bad marketing.

- You should use the product yourself because if you don't, you'll never know if you like it – and if that happens it will show through in your editorial and your readers will detect a lack of passion about the proposition.

- Endorse the product to your readership. Don't just send a sales letter to the subscriber list without first telling readers why you are enthusiastic about the product.

- You'll have some planning and researching to accomplish before you attract endorsement income but if you make the effort, the rewards are substantial. Do not be timid about approaching programme contractors on the subject of endorsement. Many of them consider it as effective as affiliate reselling.

7 – PROVIDE NICHE SOLUTIONS FOR OTHER USERS

Set yourself up as a 'complete solutions' provider for a particular industry by offering software tools, lead generation tools, articles, etc. for your designated market. Examples include subscription sites for:

- Estate agents.

- Used car dealers.

- Internet marketers.

- Insurance agents.

- Advertising agents.

- Writing circles.

- Accountants.

- Surveyors.

Your Membership is a classic example of a subscription site that is exclusively devoted to providing how-to information to internet marketers. Its breathtaking panorama of information and services includes the following:

- Email account facilities.

- Web hosting.

- Web page creation tools.

- Auto-responders.

- E-commerce instruction and tools.

- CGI tools.

- Press release service.

- Networking.

- Ezines.

- Mass mailing.

- Classified ad pages.

- Link pages.

- Search engines.

- Banner exchanges.

- Submission software and services.

- Over 1000 affiliate reseller programmes.

Go now to the *Your Membership* site and see in how many ways you could link its structure to your own conception of a subscription-based website as a profitable retirement pursuit.

www.yourmembershipwebsite.com

If you possess expert knowledge in any particular field of commercial activity, think seriously about setting yourself up as a niche solution provider on the internet. Don't worry about provision of the necessary electronic tools – you'll locate them all somewhere or other for free in cyberspace.

8 – SHARE INFORMATION ON YOUR OWN DISCUSSION BOARD

Do you have a special topic about which you feel passionate, about which you'd like to share information with others? Then set up your own discussion board on the internet and get paid for your efforts. You could of course be altruistic and do it for no reward by joining the plethora of free discussion boards on just about any topic imaginable. However, the problem with free discussion boards is that by their very nature they are prone to abuse and offer limited value to participants. Indeed, most free discussion boards are no more than glorified spam factories. Unless they are constantly 'moderated', discussion boards become a place for promoters to place their product-of-the-day link.

On the other hand, recognised experts in the particular market you are targeting will voluntarily moderate a paid-subscription-only discussion board. Participants would only be allowed to post messages and replies using their ID. Add to this the fact that all the participants have paid a fee and are therefore motivated, and you have the formula for a successful subscription-based discussion board to serve as a profitable retirement pursuit.

If you have a bee in your bonnet, set up a paid discussion board and get paid for allowing other people to let off steam. If you like people, if you like controversy, if you like discussion – this could be the online retirement business for you.

Here are three examples of very active and very profitable paid discussion boards:

The Internet Marketing Challenge

Discussion board for internet marketers where, according to the home page, subscribers (for an annual fee of £155) can obtain many features including:

1. Get your questions answered free of charge by highly-paid internet consultants, as often as you want (so you can stop spending hours or even days frustrated and hunting for answers).

2. Get your website or marketing campaign evaluated free of charge by these same highly paid experts (and find out instantly what's holding you back from online sales).

3. Be privy to insider methods for starting, promoting, and marketing your business, product, or service on the internet – methods which are simple, risk-free, and up-to-the-minute.

   www.discusware.com

The Universal Thread

Discussion board for computer programming professionals – charges a yearly fee of £60 for access.

   www.universalthread.com

The Blackjack review Network

This one is dedicated to winning at blackjack! Charges £21 annually for access.

www.bjrnet.com

9 – DEVELOP TOOLS TO SIMPLIFY ONLINE TASKS

If you have the ability to develop internet tools that could assist other users to perform tasks more easily or to simplify their lives, you have the basis for a profitable subscription-based website business. *The Ultimate Advertising Club* is an example of a classic electronic tool provider. Ninety-nine per cent of websites don't get enough targeted traffic to create any true and predictable flow of custom and this site is all about joining the one per cent who get the traffic and make the sale.

www.ultimateadvertisingclub.com

This one will work for you if you have the technical know-how to create and develop useful electronic tools.

10 – OPEN UP YOUR SITE AS A TRAINING CENTRE

This is a site that contains information and tools to help subscribers learn or enhance a particular skill. Online classes, real audio and video lessons or teleclasses are a few of the features that you could offer. *Big Stock Play* is a good example. It's a training centre for investors and offers its subscribers a variety of packages. It's worth a visit just to see what goes into planning a training centre website.

www.bigplaystocks.com

- Were you a skilled trainer in your working days?
- Are you willing to share your accumulated knowledge with others?
- Do you have the technical ability?

If so – on all three counts – then go for it. You will earn a very handsome income for your efforts.

11 – COMPILE RESOURCES AND SELL ACCESS TO THE LIST

Compile a list of resources that are employed in a particular industry and sell access to the list. There are several such subscription-based websites on the internet right now; sites relating to government contracting assignments, domain names, and classified ads. Take an early look at one such successful resource centre that sells a list of free classified ad sites.

Online Classified Club

Cyberspace resource centres are becoming increasingly popular and various categories of internet users will subscribe to those sites that offer genuine resource lists.

www.tunza-products.com/classified/ads.html

12 – CREATE AN EXCLUSIVE EZINE ARTICLE CENTRE

Ezine publishing is an exploding industry and the tens of thousands of online publishers worldwide all have one thing in common – they need a constant flow of fresh content for their publications. Combine this with the fact that there is available to you an equally constant pool of writers who would love to have their articles published – in exchange for a promotional link – and you have the potential for a great subscription-based website. If you have a thirst for information and possess highly developed organisational skills, give serious consideration to this particular way of making money on the internet. You do not need to be technically-minded to create an ezine article centre because there is ample free help available, right there on the internet. If this opportunity appeals to you, go for it, because not too many people are doing it yet. Visit www.zinos.com for a superb example on how to set up such a centre.

13 – CHARGE FOR ACCESS TO YOUR REFERRALS DIRECTORY

How's this for an idea? Offer homeowners access to a directory of reliable, recommended contractors, plumbers, electricians, painters, landscapers, handymen, etc. – and charge a fee for access to your exclusive directory. Have a look and see what this example has to offer: www.angieslist.com. *Angie's List* is a consumer-driven project that collects customer satisfaction ratings on local service companies in more than 250 categories. This referrals directory offers assistance to subscribers on an entire spectrum of homeowner headaches.

I have a retired friend who used this concept to negotiate fees on a subscription-based website for nationwide B&Bs. Internet referral directories are booming because everyone wants a one-stop source for what they want, when they want it – which is invariably, right now.

14 – PROVIDE AN INFORMATION-ON-DEMAND SERVICE

Set up a subscription-based website business to provide fast access to timely data for a designated industry, market sector or sub-sector. Companies and commercial institutions that rely on accurate, timely data are willing to pay handsomely for access to a site which guarantees up-to-date accurate information. Examples include stock, bond and commodity quotes, government contract bid requests, mortgage rates, pending legislation and government statistics. Provision of accurate, timely information is what the internet is really all about. If you can provide such information on demand, you will make money.

15 – OFFER AN ELECTRONIC PRESS RELEASE SERVICE

This is a service where you fax or email a client's press release to targeted members of the media. *The Internet Marketing Warriors* offer their members a free database of over 7,000 fax numbers and email addresses of core global media. If you are interested, go to this site for membership information.

www.thewarriorgroup.com

For more on this particular way of making money on the internet, you might also want to visit this website which offers a completely integrated one-stop press release service.

www.press-releases.net

If this way of making money online interests you, you'll find all the necessary tools at the two sites listed. Spend some time at both, choose the one you feel most comfortable with, sign up, and make a start on your new profitable retirement pursuit.

16 – CREATE A SEARCH-ENGINE-POSITIONING SERVICE

In estate agency practice the most important aspect of the marketing strategy is location, location, location. The internet equivalent to this adage is *position*, *position*, and *position*. A search engine positioning service helps clients get their websites listed towards the top of the search engine results; this higher than average positioning almost guarantees high traffic for the site. Operators of this type of service keep up with the latest tools and techniques for top positioning and employ these resources to build doorway pages that rank high on the search engine indexes.

You can find out more about search engine placement by visiting this site.

www.searchengineforums.com/bin/Ultimate.cgi

There is a learning curve required to take advantage of this opportunity but your application in mastering the skills will pay off handsomely because the demand for the service is huge – and growing.

17 – OPERATE A KEY-PHRASE-DISCOVERY SERVICE

This service examines a website and produces a list of all the keywords and keyword phrases that are relevant to the site's content. This keyword list can then be used to:

- build keyword-specific doorway pages for search-engine submission;

- advertise on pay-for-click services such as FindWhat.com;

- find link partners;

- find targeted advertising media.

The *Wordtracker* keyword search tool is of tremendous assistance in locating keywords. It lists the number of searches on the site for a particular keyword during the previous month and is a superb example of the system in action.

www.wordtracker.com

Fig. 4. The Wordtracker keyword search tool.

This is another business that requires some application on your part before you get going, but the information and tools you need are all available; just waiting for you to pull down and get started on a money-making retirement pursuit.

18 – SET UP AS A WEB GRAPHICS DESIGNER/ COPYWRITER

Let's look first at the copywriting aspect. A web page's copy and how it is laid out can make all the difference between a profitable site and one that simply exists and costs money to maintain. You can charge substantial money if you can compose copy that sells. For information on online copywriting visit this site.

www.write101.com

Do you have a talent for drawing or graphic design?

If so, you can make a good living creating graphic content and artwork. To solicit business, surf the web and find commercial sites that could use a graphics makeover. Contact the webmaster (whose address is usually featured on the home page) and offer your services. If you are good, word will spread fast and you could end up with more work than you can handle. Should you be so lucky, go out and hire someone equally talented to assist in the servicing of your increased workload. Put your native skills to the test and join the creative gravy train with your own retirement operation. Proficient writers and designers are always in demand on the internet.

19 – CASH IN ON THE LATEST ELECTRONIC BOOM

Commercial users worldwide are fast discovering the advantages the internet affords to facilitating coaching and training through interactive websites, real audio and video, and DVD software products. Here's how to exploit this exploding opportunity.

CGI programming tutorials

If you know (or take the trouble to learn) CGI (Common Gateway Interface) programming you can develop online tutorials that teach others how to write programs. You then have the choice of either selling access to the tutorials or offering them for free but selling more advanced courses. For an example of this, visit this site.

www.cgi101.com

Web connectivity tutorials

For some people it's a big deal getting their first website connected on the internet. If you have the skills to put it all together in a how-to format, users will pay to have a step-by-step guide (book, CD-ROM, video) that shows exactly what to do and which software to use.

Java tutorials

Java is the programming language to use for developing database applications online. It allows for much more flexibility, speed and bandwidth than does CGI. However, as Java is much more difficult to master than CGI, it would be best to approach this business by catering for software programmers who want to learn how to leverage their skills on the web. For example, you could create tutorials that show programmers how to establish database connectivity.

Lead-generation coaching

As long as there are sales people, there will be a demand for prospect leads, and if you can teach sellers how to generate more leads, they will beat a path to your door to get at your skills-training products. The key is to specialise in one specific industry and for lead-generation coaching you can choose from estate agents, car dealers, stockbrokers, mortgage lenders, financial advisors, etc. What you could do is to create a site that gives them some free 'taster' information and then sell them more advanced courses in the form of videos or how-to manuals. Visit this website to see how it's done.

www.leads4insurance.com

Internet marketing tutorial

There are numerous internet marketing courses on offer and the majority of these are in the form of manuals that are downloadable. Is there perhaps an opening here for a multi-video format? This animated approach could take viewers from A to Z and show them how to develop and market a website. It could also demonstrate how to use software tools, where to advertise, and how to install simple CGI scripts to boost traffic.

Sales coaching

Unlike lead-generation coaching, sales coaching does not necessarily need to be targeted to a specific market, but can teach sales techniques in general to a wide variety of sales professionals.

Weight-loss coaching

Develop a website devoted to helping people lose weight and you're on your way to creating a successful retirement business. One way to approach this opportunity is to create a referral centre to assist users to find partners in their quest to lose weight. Then you go on to sell participants weight-loss videos, menus, menu planning or even weekly teleclasses.

Health and fitness coaching

Similar to weight-loss coaching, this concept could be adapted to helping other retirees to get in shape. Offer videos and manuals on exercise, weight lifting, nutrition, etc.

Online golf coaching

Help golfers improve their game by offering free tips on driving, putting, posture, etc. – and then sell them videos, DVDs, manuals, teleclasses.

If you are an experienced programmer, training and coaching is where the money is.

20 – OFFER CREATIVE TUITION

Do you have a measure of expertise in the creative arts? It might be writing, music, figure drawing, sketching, watercolours or oil painting, etc. For example, are you a writer or better still an author with a few published titles to your credit? Then consider expanding your expertise by devising a course of instruction based on creative writing for beginners. You could market your information product via a mini website like 1st-creative-writing-course.com or use the multi-dimensional approach of www.writing-for-profit.com. The first of these sites which I designed together with the accompanying tutorial started life in October 2004 and (as I write) is ranking in the top one per cent on Alexa (www.alexa.com is the accepted source for measuring traffic performance of billions of web pages) at 74,513 out of 96,000,000+ websites. That, dare I say it, has to be exceptional for a retirement hobby venture.

Could you do something similar using your own expertise?

9
Get paid to express your opinions online

You are a virtual fountain of disparate tracts of information culled from the experiences of a lifetime. Why not get paid for expressing your opinions? This is a cushy retirement number and it pays well as you will glean from the following article. It was written by an expert on the subject and I could not do better than (with the kind permission of the author) reproduce here it in its entirety.

INCOME STREAMS: GET PAID FOR YOUR OPINION

By Rosalind Gardner Copyright © 2004

Every year, companies in the United States spend over 250 billion dollars trying to convince consumers to buy their products and services, and that's just in the USA! Although the lion's share of that money is spent on advertising, a huge amount is devoted to market research. Understanding how we as consumers think and why we choose certain products over others, enables companies to improve their goods and services. The better they understand us as consumers, the more money they make.

Because it *pays them* to know what we like and want, companies are willing to pay us for our opinions. It makes perfect business sense. Using the internet as a direct channel to ordinary people like you and me, paying for online surveys is a cheap, efficient and very effective way of gathering quality and highly targeted market research.

There are companies that will pay you up to:

- $ 99 per online survey;
- $ 250 per hour to participate in focus groups;
- $ 150 per hour to take phone surveys;
- $ 425 per hour to view movie trailers!

Online surveys are general forms generated by marketing research companies to obtain information on a particular product or service. They perform detailed investigation on the feedback they get from you and pass it on to top companies. Focus groups are meetings wherein the attendees express their opinions on a particular topic. They are generally conducted by phone or in chat rooms.

In other cases you can get paid to:

- be a Mystery Shopper;
- shop and read emails;
- drive a free car.

As a Mystery Shopper you are sent to a designated retail or commercial area to buy a product or service. You then evaluate and comment on your overall buying experience with that establishment. Some companies and advertisers pay cash for every email you read about their products. I've read about some who are doing this and making between $1,000 to $1,800 a month, no gimmicks.

No doubt you want to know about the free car. These cars have advertisements on them. Drive them, and you won't pay insurance or monthly instalments. The companies providing these vehicles earn their money from the advertising on the vehicle. Payment is made in different ways. Some companies pay instantly via PayPal, whereas others will mail you a cheque.

In lieu of cash, some companies pay with:

- Napster Music Downloads;
- Buy.com Gift Certificates.

Other companies will enter you into drawings for large cash prizes, let you earn points that can be used to buy products, or redeem for cash. Whatever the method of payment, you will be provided with the exact compensation details before you decide to participate.

Finding paid surveys online can be a time-consuming process, and there are a number of scam operators in the business. Fortunately, a few smart entrepreneurs have developed huge databases of reputable companies that are paying for online surveys. They themselves use those databases to earn all or part of their incomes.

The various databases that I researched list between 300 and up to almost 700 resources. To gain access to these databases costs a one-time membership fee of between $29.95 and $37. However, just one hour online can pay for your membership. Most accept Visa, MasterCard, American Express, Discover, Eurocard, and Visa-Debit, MasterCard-Debit, and Novus cards, PayPal and online cheques.

You have nothing to lose either. If you're not satisfied, each company offers a money back guarantee of between 60 and 90 days.

Most of these listing companies offer incentives to join such as:

- e-books;
- 250 free business cards;
- automation software;
- 2 free airline tickets;
- 3 day 2 night vacation.

Your membership will entitle you to the latest industry news and you will be generally notified when new companies join the database. Generally, the surveys are between 10 and 15 minutes in length, and although you can make up to $100 by completing one survey, $10 to $25 is far more typical. Although you probably won't get rich completing surveys, or participating in focus groups, you could make a tidy sum doing it either full or part-time. Basically, the more surveys that you complete, the more money you will make. I rather prefer stacks of $10, 15 and $25 cheques to the alternative – no cheques at all.

This great opportunity is well-suited to anyone who works from home, students, stay-at-home parents, retired people, and for those with special needs. You can do it from anywhere in the world! *And it doesn't matter if you live outside the USA. This opportunity is open to people the world over.* As long as you can cash a US dollar cheque, you can be in business.

Fig. 5. Online surveys database.

Here, listed in alphabetical order, is a list of the best online databases of survey companies.

Get Cash for Surveys

- 300+ Companies Listed

- Guarantee Terms – 90 days

- Paid Surveys Fee Range – $5–$150

- Focus Group Fee Range – up to £250

- Bonus – Automation Software
- One-time subscription fee – $37.00

  www.getcashforsurveys.com/?hop=webvista

Paid Online Surveys

- 275+ Companies Listed
- Guarantee Terms – 90 days
- Paid Surveys Fee Range – $25–$99
- Focus Group Fee Range – $30–$200
- Bonus – Copy of H0me Business Connection Magazine and Automation software
- One-time subscription fee – $34.97

  www.paid-online-surveys.com/?hop=webvista2

Paid Surveys Online

- 300+ Companies Listed
- Guarantee Terms – 90 days
- Paid Surveys Fee Range – $5–$75
- Focus Group Fee Range – $50–$150
- Other Services – $4–$25
- Bonus – 3 Day 2 Night Vacation
- One-time subscription fee – $34.95

  www.paidsurveysonline.com/?hop=webvista2

Survey Junction

- 700 Companies Listed
- Guarantee Terms – 90 days

- Paid Surveys Fee Range – $25–$99
- Focus Group Fee Range – $30–$200
- Bonus – 2 round trip airfares
- One-time subscription fee – 32.95

  www.surveyjunction.com/?hop=webvista2

Survey Scout

- 450+ Companies Listed
- Guarantee Terms – 90 days
- Paid Surveys Fee Range – $5–$120
- Focus Group Fee Range – up to $200
- Bonus – Automation software
- One-time subscription fee – $34.95

  www.surveyscout.com/?hop=webvista2

Survey Platinum

- 450+ Companies Listed
- Guarantee Terms – 90 days
- Paid Surveys Fee Range – $5–$150
- Focus Group Fee Range – up to $250
- Bonus – e-books, 250 business cards
- One-time subscription fee – $34.95

  www.survey-platinum.com/?hop=webvista2

WorkOnline4Pay

- 400 Companies Listed

- Guarantee Terms – 60 days

- Paid Surveys Fee Range – $5–$75

- Focus Group Fee Range – $50–$250

- Other Services – $4–$25

- Bonus – 2 free airline tickets

- One-time subscription fee – $29.95

www.workonline4pay.com/?hop=webvista2

Have your say, and help shape the products and services of the future. Select one or more from the Internet Online Paid Survey Database companies listed above, and start collecting steady, regular, monthly paycheck working from the comfort of home.

About the Author: Article by Rosalind Gardner, best-selling author of the *Super Affiliate Handbook: How I Made $436,797 Last Year Selling Other People's Products Online.* RosalindGardner.com

This article focused on the North American marketplace but the principles are by and large the same for participation in online surveys in the United Kingdom. Visit these six sites for a string of money-spinning opportunities that could provide you with a highly lucrative retirement pursuit.

www.apennyearned.co.uk/surveys_uk.html

www.easytorecall.com/online_surveys.htm

www.kikamoocow.worldonline.co.uk/freecash.htm

www.homebusinessuk.co.uk/surfing.htm

www.getpaidguides.com/survey/companies.html

10
Turning retirement planning into a profitable pursuit

The subject of retirement is a valuable niche in itself; hence the book you are reading and its predecessor *Your Retirement Masterplan* (How To Books 2004). Indeed, if you were to type 'retirement' into the Amazon.com search engine you'd come up with 48,515 titles on the topic – while Amazon.co.uk displays a less dramatic total of 3,014. Does that indicate overkill or worse still exploitation? Not a bit of it. Like the London buses there will be another one (retiree) along in a minute and according to the UK 2001 Census there are now for the first time ever more people over 60 than there are children.

Could you make money out of the new concept of retirement?

Perhaps you could if you put your mind to it …

In this chapter we will focus on a unique opportunity for retirees who have a background in coaching or the marketing of training services. How about a profitable retirement pursuit focused exclusively on the subject of retirement planning *per se*? Why not? You're already there and rapidly gathering information on how to make your own third age a rewarding and fulfilling experience. Why not add to your special know-how and at the same time increase your retirement income by using this mounting intelligence to help others?

There is one outstanding, professional and highly ethical opportunity currently available online and it is a review of the *Retirement Options Coaching Programme* that forms the nucleus of this brief chapter. It will cost you to participate but it will be worth it. Follow the guidelines in the marketing plan and you should recoup your investment in a very short space of time.

HOW TO BECOME A RETIREMENT COACHING EXPERT

The *Retirement Options Coaching Programme* has evolved out of the undeniable fact that the rocky financial times of the new millennium have had a pronounced impact on retirement planning. Couple this with disappointing private/company pension forecasts, and the volatility of the market is forcing many people to work a little longer than they had originally planned, or even in some instances to postpone retirement indefinitely. However, money alone does not determine the entire retirement experience and decisions need to also include the emotional aspects of quitting the workplace.

Engage in a free 'taster' to evaluate this opportunity

During a one hour introductory class you will discover why retirement coaching is among the fastest growing niche opportunities around today. You'll also learn how to acquire this competency and start coaching the 76 million baby-boomers facing retirement.

The Retirement Success Profile (RSP) is a free course and an introduction to the *Retirement Options 6-week Certification Programme*. (Website details are at the end of this chapter.)

There are 15 retirement success factors involved in this exercise:

1. Career Reorientation: Let Go ...
2. Retirement Value: Reframe Your Attitudes ...
3. Personal Empowerment: Take Charge ...
4. Physical Wellness: Grow Well ...
5. Monetary Adequacy: Find Your Wealth ...
6. Quality of Life – Present: Seek Peace ...

7. Quality of Life – Future: Have Dreams …

8. Spirituality/Meaning: Construct Purpose …

9. Respect for Leisure: Have Fun …

10. Personal Flexibility: Welcome Change …

11. Lifespan Spiritual Development: Live Now …

12. Care-giving Responsibilities: Honour Yourself …

13. Home Life: Get Connected …

14. Maturation Vitality: Become Ageless …

15. Replacement of Work Functions: Get Going …

With your own Retirement Success Profile (RSP) to hand you will have solid quantitative proof of the relevance of the material for your own life. Since the profile describes you alone, you become concretely yet intimately aware that this learning is personal; the material is not for the person sitting next to you ... it is for you. And with the specific adult learning suggestions and learning activities that flow from your personal RSP, you will not only realise that the experience is individually practical but that it opens the door to becoming qualified as a retirement coach.

THE BENEFITS OF COACHING RETIREMENT PLANNING

Capitalise on the booming retirement market by coaching individuals over 50 who are either recently retired or planning their retirement, and learn how to utilise the RSP to build your own customer base.

- **Create a new coaching opportunity with an endless supply of clients** – 76 million baby boomers are facing retirement over the next 20 years.

- **Attract new clients and extend the life of existing clients** – Become a retirement expert and coach clients (and their spouses) though a major life transition.

- **Proven programme with turn-key training and support** – This is an in-depth coaching course designed exclusively for people over 50 and it comes complete with training and support.

- **No financial planning experience required** – You will be instructing clients on life planning and strategy – not their financial planning needs.

THE MARKETPLACE FOR RETIREMENT COACHING

The Retirement Success Profile and Retirement Options Programme are both dynamic and flexible. Any coach can utilise these courses in individual, couple or group settings.

Here are a few examples:

Individual Coaching

- Anyone who is 50+ and actively planning their retirement.

- Anyone who is within ten years of working less than full time, or anyone who will receive a pension or pension-like supplemental income.

- Anyone who is retired and is looking for greater purpose and meaning in life.

The Retirement Options Programme is the most advanced pre-retirement planning course available. It has been administered to thousands of individuals who realised their third age strategy through the RSP and Retirement Options Programme.

Couples Coaching

Nowadays married couples move into retirement together and whether a spouse is employed or not, both can benefit immensely from retirement coaching. The Retirement Options Programme is an excellent way to bring a couple together for personal coaching. It has been administered to thousands of married couples over the past ten years with excellent results.

Group Coaching

- Continuing Education Programmes.

- Professional and/or Trade Associations.

- Government Agencies – National and/or Local.

- Church or Religious Organisations.

- Financial Planning Organisations.

TRAINING FOR RETIREMENT COACHING CERTIFICATION

This involves six weeks of interactive, focused one-hour group TeleClass training comprised of lecture, questions and discussion led by Joanne Waldman M.Ed. and Dr Richard Johnson, Founder and Creator of *Retirement Options*.

- *Class 1*: Introduction/Overview.

- *Class 2*: Assessment Review.

- *Class 3*: RSP **Factor Review 1–5**: work re-orientation, attitude towards retirement, health perception, financial security.

- *Class 4*: RSP **Factor Review 6–10**: current and projected life satisfaction, life meaning, leisure interests, adaptability.

- *Class 5*: RSP **Factor Review 11–15**: life stage satisfaction, dependents, relationship issues, perception of age, replacement of work function.

- *Class 6*: **Focus Person Review**.

- Participant Certification Exam – **Certification** – RSP Trained Retirement Coach.

TeleClass training materials

- *Coach's Training Manual* – Course outline, over 100 powerful questions and 30 exercises for ongoing use.

- *The NEW Retirement Book* – Programme companion book with expanded RSP information and how-to guide to create Personal Retirement Mission Statement and Retirement Options Strategy Plan for your reference and use with clients.

- *Coach's Training Audiotapes* – Eight-tape Audio Programme includes a Retirement Options seminar for ongoing reference and consultation.

Free Additional Marketing and Support

- Client Referrals – RSP Training listing on www.retirementoptions.com.

- Marketing – 'RSP Training' buttons and banners for your website.

- Monthly e-Newsletter.

- Ongoing email and phone support.

One-off cost for qualification

Your total investment for this TeleClass Programme and accompanying course materials amounts to a single payment of $495 USD (approx. £275).

Full details of the *Retirement Options Coaching Programme* are available at this website www.retirementoptions.com and even if you've never been involved in coaching of any description, this unique, highly imaginative and profitable retirement pursuit might still be worth checking out.

Despite the undoubted profitability and fulfilment factors attaching thereto, the concept of retirement coaching has restricted appeal, but in the chapter coming up we'll be looking at another opportunity of a general nature that is demonstrating incredible popularity among today's retirees.

11
Why so many retirees use eBay to make money

More and more retirees are turning to eBay for their profitable pursuit because it doesn't take a genius to make money with online auctions, nor does it require participants to have any specialised computer knowledge. You don't even need to be a skilled entrepreneur because eBay does most of the work for you. With over 1.5 billion page views per month and more than 1,000 categories, they bring customers directly to you and save on heavy advertising costs. Your job is to make a successful sales pitch to those internet users who see your auctions *but doing that isn't as easy as some people think.* You will be competing with more than two million other virtual auction sellers, many of whom are veterans at online marketing and highly knowledgeable in the niche markets that abound on eBay.

So how do you compete with them? The answer is simple: **inside information**.

GAINING AN EDGE ON ONLINE AUCTION COMPETITORS

This chapter provides you with all the information needed to get ahead on eBay and gives you an instant edge over your competitors. It lays bare the insider secrets on eBay trading – and if you follow the advice set out in these pages, you will be armed with the knowledge necessary for an extremely lucrative home-based retirement business buying or selling virtually anything via online auctions.

THE ESSENTIALS FOR GETTING STARTED

A computer, an internet connection, an open mind, and a modicum of intelligence are the essentials. But you will also need to be familiar with the eBay format and understand the basic functions of listing items on the online auction site.

Some questions that require answers before you start

- What do you want to sell and why?
- To whom do you want to sell?
- Will your product appeal to everyone, or only to a select niche market?
- Are your potential customers pre-qualified for your product?
- Where can you obtain your product?
- How popular is your product?
- What is the age-range and income-range of your potential customers?

DECIDING WHAT TO SELL ON EBAY

With over 1,000 categories, you can market virtually anything on eBay but choosing what to sell can be overwhelming. My advice is to look first to your own retirement hobbies and interests because the most successful sales pitch almost always comes from the heart. If you don't believe in what you're selling and you aren't willing to stand behind your product, your retirement online auctions business will certainly fail. You should never sell a product that you aren't enthusiastic about – but if you do, you'd best fake your enthusiasm like an accomplished actor or your offer will prove to be a complete turnoff. Either way, you must pass on positive energy about your product to prospective buyers.

It is true that some things sell better than others. Information and software are particularly hot sellers because almost all computer users are pre-qualified for those products. In other words, *the fact that they are using a computer means they need software, and the fact that they are using the information superhighway means they are already looking for information.* Selling to a pre-qualified market can be very profitable, but you must be enthusiastic about what you're selling or it will surely fail.

FINDING YOUR NICHE MARKET

Once you have a product in mind you will require to pinpoint your niche market. This is very easy to do. Brainstorm a list of interests, hobbies, topics, subjects, and ideas that are similar or related to your product. For example, if you sell knives then you would consider the following interests/hobbies relevant to your product: camping, hiking, hunting, fishing, boating, knife collecting, diving, martial arts, sporting goods, kitchenware, cutlery, tools, collectible hand tools, etc. The eBay users who visit such categories on the auction site make up your niche market.

Once you know where your customers go, you need to know their preferences.

Undertake a second brainstorming session to create a list of their interests, hobbies, likes and dislikes, age range, income potential, likely vocation, marital status, etc. Devise a complete dossier on your potential customers in that niche market. The reason for this will become clear later as you learn to write an effective sales pitch. The sales pitch aims at attracting a certain profile of eBay user and is the most profitable tool you can use to increase the percentage sales of your products.

CHOOSING A CATEGORY OR CATEGORIES

You've put a lot of thought into your product and completed the initial phase of getting started. You're excited about your merchandise and you're ready to start selling it on eBay. The next step is to find your *precise* niche market as it applies to online auctions. This refers to the category in which you will list your item(s). Considering eBay has over 1,000 categories to choose from, this should be a relatively easy process but there is one important three-point strategy you should know about. Before listing your item in any category, follow these simple steps:

1. First, browse through all of the categories and write down which ones you feel are relevant to your product. You should be able to find at least 5–10 possible choices.

2. Next, write down the number of auctions currently online in each of those categories (the number of auctions online will appear next to the category name). An average in any category is about 1,000, so if there are more than 1,000 you may conclude that the category is active and if there are fewer than 1,000 you may consider it inactive. I consider categories with over 3,000 auctions to be popular and those with over 10,000 the most popular.

3. Using this ranking system, rate the categories that you have chosen for your product. I recommend listing in active categories only because they get the most traffic. If you put your product in an inactive section of eBay, you may get few or no bids, even if you feature it. Avoid categories with fewer than 1,000 auctions online.

KEEPING TRACK OF YOUR AUCTIONS

Once you have more than 5–10 auction listings online you must develop an effective system for keeping track of them all. Simply logging the items and sending a confirmation email to the winners is not enough. For example, if a customer purchases one of your products and asks whether you have received payment or not, you need to track down the item number to confirm remittance. Other customers may want to know when the item was shipped or they may have questions about auctions won in the past.

The easiest way to keep track of your auctions and perform a complete market analysis on your products is with *Auction Master 2000*. Here's a tip. Join in an eBay auction and get it for a fraction of the list price. The last time I looked, an auction for the software had just started with an opening bid of 99 cents. Just three days later it went for $3.99 – a saving of $26 (approx. £14).

Should you list fewer than 5–10 auctions at a time you can probably keep track of them with pen and paper or a simple spreadsheet. If you choose this method, follow these steps for keeping track of the auctions:

- Use a separate sheet of paper for each auction you list.

- Write down the item number, URL, listing date, listing price, and category, along with any other comments or pertinent information.

- When the auction ends, make a note of the ending date, the sale price and the buyer's contact information.

- Index the auctions by number in a file for quick reference.

Selling the merchandise is only half the battle – you *must* keep track of your sales or you will quickly find yourself lost and confused.

WHY A PICTURE IS WORTH A THOUSAND WORDS ON EBAY

An essential aspect of every eBay auction in which a physical product is sold (excluding services, digitised information, or software) is an **image file**. Hardly anyone is willing to buy what they cannot see. If your competitor displays an impressive picture of a product and you don't, then you lose business. It's that simple.

All you will need is a digital camera and somewhere to host your graphic output such as a directory in an internet website or a special image hosting company. (I recommend www.o-f.com – this service is both reliable and inexpensive). Incidentally, eBay has extensive help files on how to attach a picture to your auction – and it really isn't difficult.

Highlighting the best features of your produce

The chosen image should be used to highlight the best features of your product but make sure that the lighting and the setup is correct, that you take the time to produce a high-quality illustration. When browsing through auctions, invariably the image is the first thing to attract potential customers, so the more effort you put into presenting outstanding digital pictures the more profitable your business will be. Indeed, if you are selling a physical product don't even think about listing it on eBay until you have a quality picture to attach to your auction. The picture sells – better than a thousand words.

DEVELOPING YOUR SALES STRATEGY

The key to making profits on eBay is to develop a detailed and efficient strategy long before you list your first item. First you need to know what type of product you want to sell, where to find your niche market, and develop a profile of your average customer. In addition, you should also have determined which categories are appropriate for your produce. Now you are ready to set your strategy for the business; a strategy that you can apply to virtually any product you wish to sell on eBay. Fill in the specifics as they relate to your own particular niche market and merchandise.

There are two types of seller on eBay

High Volume and *Low Volume*; high volume sellers are those who list more than 10 auctions online at a time; low volume sellers keep fewer than 10 auctions online at a time.

The profit margin determines into which category you will fit

For example, if you were to sell property and make, say £5,000 per sale, you might only need to list a few properties each week to make huge profits. The same applies for expensive jewellery, motor cars, and other items with a large profit margin. However, if you sell magazines subscriptions or other inexpensive items you may only make £5/£10 per sale. In this case, you would need to list dozens or even hundreds of items at a time to attract an acceptable level of profits and you would thus become a high volume seller.

I know what you're thinking. Why would anyone go through the effort of listing so many items when it seems so easy to catalogue a few large items and make a fortune? The answer cuts to the heart of internet selling itself: current eBay research confirms that *buyers prefer to spend under £35 for a product when they engage in online auctions.* This makes sense. Would you pay thousands for something you have never seen? Another reason for opting to be a high volume seller is that it is easy to buy inexpensive items at wholesale prices but almost impossible to acquire property or motor cars at wholesale prices.

Armed with this information, you must consider the product you're selling and make an intelligent, informed decision on whether to become a high or low volume seller. You have plenty of free time to devote to your profitable retirement pursuit, so I recommend you opt for the high volume option. However, if you wish to dip your toe in the water, become an eBay seller at nights and weekends and start off with the low volume option until your business really takes off.

Again, only you know best which status to choose based on the amount of time you have available and the profit margin of your chosen merchandise. Once you determine what type of seller you will be you are half-way to developing a sales strategy.

PROJECTING YOUR STRATEGY INTO THE FUTURE

The next step is to integrate everything you have learned so far and project your selling strategy into the future. For example, let's assume you have decided to sell inexpensive fad jewellery on eBay. Here is a test case for consideration: You have identified your niche market and found the associated categories. You know that your buyers will probably spend between £7 and £15 per purchase and you realise that working on an overall margin of 30 per cent the average profit of your auctions will £3.30. You have plenty of time to devote to your retirement pursuit so you decide to become a high volume seller and choose to list 100 auctions per week.

You estimate that 70 per cent of your auction will end with winning bids – which is the eBay average. Based on this prediction, you calculate your weekly income at £231. Using *Auction Master 2000*, you plan to keep track of your auctions and use the built-in market analysis feature to discontinue unpopular items and re-list the popular ones.

- You have a wholesale account set up with a jewellery supplier and have already purchased enough stock to cover your first week of eBay sales.

- You plan to re-list every auction as soon as it ends and place one weekly order to fill your inventory along with one weekly outgoing mailing to your buyers.

- Your basic sales strategy is set and you are ready to begin listing your auctions.

In the example above, you've thought out *everything* before listing a single item, making sure that you are prepared for the task ahead.

Before beginning, you should project your sales strategy into the future and run through all possible problems, resolving them in your mind. If it helps, write out a paragraph like the one above and analyse it for errors of logic.

TESTING OUT YOUR STRATEGY BEFORE YOU BEGIN

List all of your auctions as **regular** auctions before you begin. Do not feature them or use the 'Dutch Auction' option at this time. Test out your sales strategy and evaluate the popularity of your product in its niche market for several weeks before continuing.

TO FEATURE OR NOT TO FEATURE

Featured eBay auctions show up at the top of the item's category main page. This ensures that anyone who visits that category will probably see your auction, as the average browser scrolls down a few screens and then leaves.

Featured auctions get more bids but they also cost more – a lot more. Before deciding whether or not to feature an item, you need to evaluate its popularity. You should perform basic rule of thumb market analysis or alternatively, obtain a more accurate evaluation by using *Auction Master 2000* software.

I recommend listing your item in its category if it has an average sales percentage of 50 per cent or greater. In other words, after running regular auctions for a few weeks, you should choose the 'featured in category' option if more than half of the auctions for that item have ended in a sale. Choose the **boldface** title option whenever you feature one of your items; it draws more attention to your product.

ACCESS TRAINING AND MERCHANDISE TO SELL ON EBAY

Everyone knows about eBay but most people aren't aware that there are over 25,000 people in the UK earning a full-time living from it – just buying-and-selling items over the internet for a profit. There's a special online report available that provides comprehensive training and access to sources for merchandise to buy at wholesale and then resell on eBay. You'll find the website address at the foot of this section.

eBay top sellers' secret revealed

Most people think 'I could never do that' but the secret is that a lot of items being sold on eBay aren't even owned by the people selling them. They're sold through drop-shipping at wholesale prices. In other words, with a list of ready-to-sell products available from these wholesale sources, the sellers list the produce on eBay – and when an item sells they send a cheque for the wholesale price of the item to the drop-ship company, who then mails the product directly to the winning bidder. Until now these wholesale sources and top-secret bidding techniques were only known to a handful of elite online sellers, but that's all changed.

This report reveals the sources

'I made over $800 in one weekend selling stuff on eBay that I bought on eBay! That's $800 profit.' – Shannon Tolle

'We're making $720 a week in our retirement on eBay' – George and Ethel Bainbridge

The report has a one-time fee of $19 (approx. £10.50) and is available for download at this site:

www.usnetnews.com/ebay/index.cgi?trffxeb2142.

Fig. 6. How to make a living from eBay.

HANDY TOOLS TO HELP YOU BUILD YOUR AUCTION BUSINESS

Time Blaster search software allows you to set up and save eBay searches that it will run at set times during the week. This software can even create a gallery of items matching your search and keep track of auctions you're interested in. It's similar to *Auction Master 2000* but more expensive to operate in the long run.

> *Website*: www.timeblaster.com/tbeindex.shtml.
> *Cost*: free 30-day trial, then £22 per year.

Auction Sniper is a clever online tool that acts on your behalf as a super-quick, all-seeing middleman. It bids to win right at the last second, so you don't encourage a bidding war and drive up the price. This is a nifty piece of software for the dedicated retiree player.

> *Website*: www.auctionsniper.com.
> *Cost*: free for your first three bids, then one per cent of each
> winning bid thereafter.

eBay Turbo Lister helps you create seductive item descriptions with a simple desktop HTML editor.

> *Website*: pages.ebay.co.uk/turbo_lister/download.html.
> *Cost*: free.

Incamail is a free web mail service offering another way to keep track of your auctions without enduring the 'My eBay' login palaver.

> *Website*: www.incamail.com.
> *Cost*: free.

eBay Toolbar reminds you which auction you're following and alerts you shortly before it ends.

> *Website*: pages.ebay.co.uk/ebay_toolbar/index.html.
> *Cost*: free.

12
Why some retirees opt for affiliate reselling

We've touched on the matter several times and now we will undertake an in-depth review of the entire concept of affiliate reselling to determine its suitability for a profitable online retirement pursuit. Those retirees who already tread this path do so because they reckon it fulfils the basic requirements for successful internet marketing: it is *passive, residual, and has the propensity to create multiple streams of income*. While it is certainly all of this don't expect to make a fortune out of affiliate reselling; only 'super' affiliates manage that. You'll be doing well if you earn pin money to begin with. This is drip feed marketing and it takes time and patience to build up steam.

WHAT IS AFFILIATE RESELLING?

In a nutshell: for affiliate reselling read virtual sales agency. There are literally thousands of commercial concerns operating on the internet who will grant you an agency and remunerate you on a commission basis to represent them and sell their produce through your own cyberspace marketing applications. In effect, the term 'affiliate reseller' is simply universally accepted internet jargon for sales agent.

Although the concept was first introduced by a purveyor of tangible merchandise (Amazon Books) the produce is mainly information packages and participants make money in one of three ways:

• Selling the product online.

- Recruiting others to do likewise.

- Combination of both.

These information packages (as evidenced in a recent Harvard Business School survey) centre on inducements to lifestyle enhancement: education, how-to, self-help, etc.

THE BENEFITS OF PARTICIPATION

Many established home-based business operators start out as affiliate resellers; some remain so, while others put the accumulated knowledge they glean from handling other people's business to developing an idea of their own.

There's a flexibility surrounding affiliate reselling that makes it an attractive proposition for newcomers to the internet. Servicing several reliable and profitable programmes can evolve in time into a business in its own right while still enabling the reseller to use the learning curve the concept provides as a stepping stone to bigger things.

Why so many people set out on their internet adventure as affiliate resellers can be summarised as follows:

- There is no long term commitment.

- You can join many of these programmes free of charge.

- Where fees are applicable, they are usually modest and sometimes refundable.

- There are no trade restrictions.

- You may take on as many opportunities as you wish.

- There is no requirement to buy stock for resale.

- Marketing strategies and tools are provided free of charge.

- There is no personal contact with prospects and customers.

- Commission statistics are normally available in real time online.

- Reimbursement is monthly by cheque or direct debit.
- No cash handling.
- No creditors.
- No debtors.

What to look out for before committing to a reseller opportunity

Visit the website and check out the credentials. Just one visit will suffice. If it's a professional operation it will display most if not all of the attributes listed above. For examples of how proven affiliate reseller programmes present their case, take a look at the sites for *Marketing Tips*, *Active Marketplace*, *Six Figure Income*, *Site Sell*, and the other opportunities listed a little further on in this chapter.

What to avoid like the plague

Disregard all 'downline' clubs (see Appendix for precise definition) offering reseller status. All they will do for you is have you work hard in contributing to a giant list of prospects which they will go out and sell to some other concern.

HOW AFFILIATE RESELLING WORKS IN PRACTICE

Operating a responsible affiliate programme is very simple. You are only replicating a formula already being successfully used by the company itself. Training is provided together with a host of electronic tools to enable you to be up and running almost immediately.

Professional concerns (such as the 10 recommended in this chapter) will set you up with all of the following:

- Multi-page website (often personalised).
- Hyperlinks and/or banners to your own personal site.

- Training manual.
- Tips on how to get the best out of your marketing.
- Essential tools.
- Secure ordering facility.
- Private members area (company news, updates, developments, etc.).
- Online commission tracking.
- Email contact.
- User name and password for confidentiality.

Ignore any opportunities you come across that do not provide these features because they are not worth consideration.

Why these features are so important

1. The multi-page website is identical in every respect to that of the programme contractor and while it may be personalised with your ID, it contains all the facilities of the home site, i.e. full product range, secure ordering and merchant account facilities, email contact, etc. All sales recorded are credited to you.

2. If you have your own website and opt instead to place a hypertext link or banner to promote the affiliate programme, you still have access to the full product range and ordering facilities. As soon as a prospect hits the link or banner, he/she is instantly transported to the programme's fully automated home site where you are credited with the link and any ensuing action, i.e. a sale.

Before you start on promotion

Familiarise yourself with every aspect of the programme, the product or service, and the market at which it is aimed. If you spend some time on this before you start on promotional activities, the copy for your own particular slant on the sales message will flow more easily and you'll be able to answer any otherwise awkward questions thrown at you by prospects. You won't be interfacing with prospects but they can reach you through the contact point at the website or in reply to your promotional emails.

Be prepared before you leap in.

Devising your marketing strategy

Affiliate reseller programmes provide a basic marketing plan for the use of all participants, but to steal a march on the hundreds of others working the same proposition, you would do well to devise your own marketing strategy. Here is a rundown on the tools you should be using to create an edge on fellow resellers.

- Search engines.
- Email marketing.
- Discussion groups.
- Classified advertising.
- Free reports.
- Banners.
- Articles.
- Signature messages.
- Promotional CD/DVD.

Always remember that you'll be open for business 24 hours a day, but your website cannot do it all on its own. It needs help from every relevant tool to nudge its message towards prospects.

The value of links and banners

If you already have a website of your own and you join a reseller programme that offers either a hyperlink or a banner routed to the main promotional site, be sure to take up the invitation. Casual surfers use these unique routed links on impulse and every time one of them makes a purchase from your hyperlink or banner, you get credit for the sale – and the commission. Routed hyperlinks can also be included in your email marketing for other propositions. While not as popular as they once were, banners are still effective when used sparingly.

Building up and using 'downlines' to effect

Stay clear of so-called downline clubs, but with judicious email marketing you can build up your own exclusive list of like-minded opportunity seekers. You may only attract a couple of dozen or so recruits in your early months of trading but if you promote consistently the numbers will increase in time to hundreds if not thousands. This is how practitioners become 'super affiliates', producing sales well above the average on every proposition they market. Add to that the additional split-level commissions earned on every piece of produce sold by *your own* downline members.

Increase revenues of existing products and services

The reason why many online operators remain in affiliate reselling after they've launched their own business is because advertising these opportunities for free is the easiest way to attract prospects to the primary business interest. When someone responds to an affiliate ad the opportunity is presented to strike up a virtual dialogue and introduce the prospect to the main source of business.

Using the affiliate product or service yourself

Use the merchandise yourself where there is a repeat purchase factor in evidence. Order the product or service direct from your own website and the commission earned will represent a substantial saving on an already discounted price.

WHY MLM ISN'T A DIRTY WORD ON THE INTERNET

In conventional networking the term MLM (multi level marketing) has certain unfortunate connotations attached to it. This is not necessarily true online. In fact MLM forms the backbone of all the affiliate reseller programmes you will encounter in searching for opportunities. If you decide not to participate in multi level marketing in your retiree internet operation, you may risk putting a severe curb on your earning power.

But what exactly is multi level marketing?

Look upon MLM as cyclical selling; selling with many layers attached to it. It is not unlike the steps in an escalator: what goes down invariably comes back up.

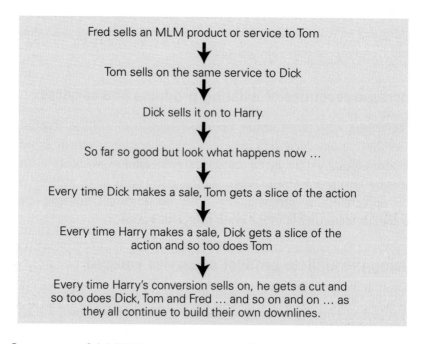

Fred sells an MLM product or service to Tom

Tom sells on the same service to Dick

Dick sells it on to Harry

So far so good but look what happens now ...

Every time Dick makes a sale, Tom gets a slice of the action

Every time Harry makes a sale, Dick gets a slice of the action and so too does Tom

Every time Harry's conversion sells on, he gets a cut and so too does Dick, Tom and Fred ... and so on and on ... as they all continue to build their own downlines.

In a successful MLM operation, the selling and earning process is never-ending. It neither levels off nor does it flatten out.

In e-commerce, one sale creates another because what you will be doing in effect is replicating your own efforts many times over (through others) as you effortlessly build your lists. That's the way it works on the internet and that's why all of the major programmes encourage and foster MLM among their affiliate members.

The benefits are threefold:

1. You build your downlines without ever having to interface with the participants.

2. You are credited with a percentage of their earnings on levels scaling from 1–10 according to the nature of individual propositions.

3. You are relieved of the responsibility of collecting monies personally because the programme contractors handle that onerous task and remunerate you monthly by cheque or direct debit.

All the time, of course, you are also earning in your own right through your own personal promotional efforts.

- MLM is good for your internet business.

- Make money from your own promotional activities.

- Build your downlines effortlessly.

- Earn additional income on a range of affiliate levels.

UNDERTAKE AN OBJECTIVE OVERVIEW

If by now you feel you might like to try your hand at affiliate reselling, you ought first to undertake an objective view of the sheer range of opportunities available globally. You can accomplish this easily by spending some time at a unique website that lists over 3,000 affiliate reseller programmes.

www.AssociatePrograms.com

Look first at the categories, choose one of particular interest, and then review a dozen or so relevant sites.

REVIEWING 10 PROVEN OPPORTUNITIES

It follows quite naturally then that the top affiliate programmes reflect the most popular opportunity categories. The programmes listed below have all been around for some years, and they are tried and tested favourites among global opportunity seekers. You may already have visited several of these sites. If not, you should make a point of looking over all of them as soon as possible. Where potential income is indicated, bear in mind though that no two people will have the same experience. The amounts you earn are down to how much time and effort you are prepared to put in.

Information product

How To Corporation *

I'll start you off with an opportunity that has only been around for three years but is already wildly successful because not only is the produce quite superb value for money but also the fact that owner Michael Green really knows how to look after his growing army of affiliate resellers. For a start he pays you back half the proceeds when you make a sale and the support and tools he provides are unrivalled. With 20 fast-selling products at your disposal (with more to follow) and 50 per cent commission a throw it would be hard not to add to your basic retirement income with this outstanding opportunity. It's free to join and here are some examples from the range, consisting of information produce and software:

How To Write A Newsletter toolkit
    www.howtocorp.com/sales.php?offer=writing333&pid=1

Easy Ezine Toolkit
    www.howtocorp.com/sales.php?offer=writing333&pid=6

Ezine Editors List
    www.howtocorp.com/sales.php?offer=writing333&pid=35

---

* Please note that this company is **not** related to the publishers of this book.

How to Create & Make a Presentation toolkit
www.howtocorp.com/sales.php?offer=writing333&pid=11

How To Corp Homepage
www.howtocorp.com/sales.php?offer=writing333&pid=15

How To PDF Creator
www.howtocorp.com/sales.php?offer=writing333&pid=16

How To Find Happiness toolkit
www.howtocorp.com/sales.php?offer=writing333&pid=20

Create and SELL Products ONLINE toolkit
www.howtocorp.com/sales.php?offer=writing333&pid=30

Create-A-Product-Seminar
www.howtocorp.com/sales.php?offer=writing333&pid=18

Easy-Download Protector toolkit
www.howtocorp.com/sales.php?offer=writing333&pid=40

Corporate Email Policy
www.howtocorp.com/sales.php?offer=writing333&pid=45

Corporate Internet Policy
www.howtocorp.com/sales.php?offer=writing333&pid=47

How To Start A Forum
www.howtocorp.com/sales.php?offer=writing333&pid=50

Start A Forum – Mini-Course
www.howtocorp.com/sales.php?offer=writing333&pid=53

How To Achieve The Swing In Golf
www.howtocorp.com/sales.php?offer=writing333&pid=28

The Meaning of Dreams
www.howtocorp.com/sales.php?offer=writing333&pid=33

How To Promote A Product
www.howtocorp.com/sales.php?offer=writing333&pid=22

This final link sends you to the How To Internet Marketer Forum: www.howtocorp.com/sales.php?offer=writing333&pid=54

Stop Trying To Promote Your Product (or service) The Hard Way! Here's How To Take Absolutely Any Online Product And Turn It Into A Booming Best Seller Today...

"In Just 2½ Minutes Time You Can Own The 24 Proven Power Keys Guaranteed To Sell Any Product (or service) On The Net!"

Looking To Promote Your Product On The Net?
Just Follow Michael Green's Proven Formula And BAM...
You've Just Turned Your Own Product Into A Money Making Best-Seller!

These 24 Power Keys work whether you are an experienced marketer or a complete "newbie".

This system works whether you are promoting a Product OR a Service.

These 24 Power Keys work no matter what it is that you are trying to sell online.

Fig. 7. How to promote a product.

Active Marketplace

Personally orchestrated by Declan Dunn, a multi-millionaire internet guru in his own right, *Winning the Affiliate Game* is the system you will be selling in his free-to-join programme. 50 per cent commission is available on your own sales, 10 per cent on those of your downline: www.activemarketplace.com.

This is an extremely popular product with opportunity seekers and one that consistently attracts favourable media coverage. You would do well to purchase it yourself before going on to sell the programme to others. It's a complete learning curve on how to be a successful reseller. Sample the product first and after a short settling-in period you could be earning between £100 and £200 per month.

Six Figure Income

Brainchild of Gery Carson, yet another internet high flier, the SFI wealth creation study course is currently operating in 140 countries worldwide. There is no cost to enrol and the programme features a 'quick-pay' compensation plan that pays out 65 per cent on the first three levels: www.sixfigureincome.com/?122341.

Potential earnings: around £200 per month.

Communications

Hosting.com

Features a breathtaking 22-page website reselling what many experts consider the finest range of virtual servers on the internet. This is a prestigious communications programme and remunerates affiliates in two ways: commission on direct sales of produce, commission on recruitment of downline affiliates. Free to join – but you'll need to demonstrate some basic product knowledge before they'll let you in on their secrets to making money, i.e. you are asked to sit an online exam: www.hosting.com.

This one is a slow burner to begin with and although many experienced resellers command huge commission payouts, do not expect to earn more than £50 per month for some considerable time.

Internet training

Site Sell

This programme would fit equally well under the 'information' category and it's one of the best opportunities online. Affiliates earn excellent commission reselling a 600-page e-book *My Site Sells* (MYSS) which contains astonishing information on how to galvanise the average website into a top money spinner. Strongly recommended opportunity and free to join: www.sitesell.com/interactive1.html.

Another slow burner that depends on drip-feed for sales. However if you stick rigidly to the marketing plan, sales will come, and a potential monthly income of £30 to £50.

Marketing Tips

Corey Rudl started his internet business from a tiny room, made some mistakes as we all do in the beginning, learned from them, and is now turning over $7.6 million annually. He put his accumulated knowledge to good use when he devised *Marketing Tips* – a remarkable opportunity that offers online newcomers a series of free lessons which he previously sold for $147 (approx. $89). Take advantage of his generosity and if you decide to sign up for his full-scale programme he will teach you how to make a great deal of money on the web. Visit this website:www.howtoproducts-xl.com and scroll down the right hand column to view a selection of Cory's famous top-selling merchandise.

Profits Vault

This one is an Aladdin's Cave of cyberspace information products; e-books, reports, courses of instruction – and how to sell them in a series of easy-to-digest learning curves. There's a one-time subscription fee of around $30 (approx. £17) which opens up the way to multiple income streams with detailed instructions on successful application. Even if you decide not to invest, you will still be offered several free courses of valuable instruction on how to implement the essential aspects of internet marketing. Here's the site and it's well worth a visit: www.profitsvault.com.

Educational

BizOpAlliance

If you're new to affiliate marketing, this is the site for you. Earn as you learn from the professionals. Free to join: www.bizoppalliance.com.

Payment processing

Clickbank

The online banking system that offers a range of services: secure ordering, merchant status, etc. Worth joining – and no fee: www.clickbank.com.

Books

Amazon

This famous online bookseller will provide you with a link to their website for free. Worth considering for the name alone; no fee required: www.amazon.com.

WHY IT'S BEST TO CAST THE NET WIDE

Why would anyone run several of these affiliate programmes at the same time?

Why not?

- The investment is modest.

- It costs nothing to service them.

- They're not cluttering up your computer.

- They're working 24 hours a day, every day.

It will pay you in the early days to review as many opportunities as you can find, sign up for those that appeal to you, and run with all of them for a time: perhaps as much as 12 months. You see, when you start out, you have no idea as to which types of programme will work best for you, when they work, or even why they work. There's also a seasonal aspect to some of them. Although wealth creation programmes are popular all year round, they peak twice a year: at the beginning of January and at the close of the holiday season when opportunity seekers get a rush of blood to the head, probably brought about by the thought of impecunious times ahead. Online dating service programmes start buzzing at the outset of spring.

You have to cast your net far and wide, hedge your bets, take note of individual programme progress, and allow time to run out its course. Look at it this way. While you are monitoring the entire spectrum of, say, six affiliate programmes in your portfolio, and each of them turned over only £20 per month, your computer would be effortlessly providing you with **additional monthly income of £120**. Some of these programmes you will discard in time, others will develop into regular income generators, and one of them might even make you wealthy.

• Evaluate every opportunity you come across.

• Sign up for as many as appeal to you.

• Test them all out on a trial basis.

• Take note of seasonal variations.

• Earn while you learn.

WHAT HAPPENS IF YOU DECIDE TO SPECIALISE STRAIGHTAWAY?

You run the risk of early disillusion with your project if you do because the odds of spotting a winner straight off are minimal. Some opportunities seem sexier than others (it's all to do with presentation) and you'll come across one where you think: this is it; this is the one, drop everything else and go for it. Don't be tempted. Stick with them all for a time because it might be one of the boring ones that pays off best in the end.

• Don't be unduly swayed by the packaging;

• Some apparently boring opportunities work best.

How come they let you join for free?

Whenever I'm asked what it costs to set up as a home-based internet operator and I reply, 'Nothing,' the response is invariably, 'I don't believe you. There has to be a catch. No one gives anything away for nothing'. That's true – no commercial concern ever really gives anything away for free. But there's no catch, only a very good reason for the magnanimity of the programme contractors.

Promotion is the key

Concerted, consistent, continuous global promotion is so vital to the reseller programme contractors that they gladly and freely dispense pre-designed, personalised websites, email facilities, auto-responders, search engines, submission tools, and free entry to their programmes when they could easily charge at least a token fee for all of this. Why? Because every time you send out a promotional email, place free classified ads, submit website addresses to the search engines and blast out your automated messages to enquirers, you are not just marketing your own little enterprise, essentially you are marketing and promoting *their* corporate programmes.

- It's win-win with the free stuff.
- Something for you, something for the programme.

Promotion is king on the internet.

LEARNING FROM THE COMPETITION

You can learn and accumulate an enormous amount of valuable information about money-making opportunities from the competition: not only from emails but also from the millions of classified ads on the internet. Take time out to study some of these and take note of those opportunities you haven't come across in your own searches. Look too at how other operators promote their propositions, the media they use, and how they compose their sales messages. Some of the copy platforms are questionable, some downright naïve, but some will inspire you and prompt you to look more closely at your own approach. Promotion is what it's all about and the ability to compose compelling sales copy is the key.

- Look at what the competition are offering.

- Observe their marketing methods.

- Learn from the good and the bad in their ad copy approach.

MAINTAINING ESSENTIAL RECORDS

As the information begins to build on your findings, you'll want to devise a simple system to keep track of it all and to allow for ready access in various circumstances. If this measure is not instigated at an early stage, it can all run away from you very quickly. There's too much of it to carry around in your head and if lost or misplaced, it will take time and cause you unnecessary aggravation in the retrieval of information. Although your business will be managed through electronic data applications, I recommend a hard copy register to house all of this essential stuff, because that will allow you to refer to your findings when you're not at your computer.

Which categories of data will this register contain?

- Income-generating websites.

- Functional websites (i.e. virtual office suites).

- Classified ad websites.

- Sites under construction (i.e. composite sites you are currently building).

- Email addresses.

- Auto-responder facilities.

- Commission scales (for individual opportunities).

- User names and passwords (e.g. for access to revenue statistics on individual programmes).

- Advertisement submission tools.

- Schedule of promotion (e.g. daily/weekly ad + email postings).

STEPS AND STAIRS TO AFFILIATE RESELLING

1. People use the internet as a source of free information but they'll also pay for it if the product promises enhancement of lifestyle.

2. Look for products that fulfil this promise.

3. Choose several opportunities from the main product categories and run with them all for a time on a pilot basis.

4. It is a mistake to throw all your energies behind one opportunity until you are convinced of its effectiveness.

5. Promotion is germane to success on the internet and that is why the reseller contractors give so much away for free in return for a promise from you on promotional activity.

6. Learn from the competition: capitalise on what they're doing right and avoid repeating their mistakes.

HOW TO GET A MULTI-RESELLER WEB BUSINESS FOR FREE

Now here's a stunning offer should you decide that your path to a profitable retirement lies in affiliate reselling. It beggars belief – but it's true. Take advantage of this free deal and your retirement money-maker plan will become a reality within fifteen minutes. Just sign up for as many affiliate programmes as you wish (that's free too) and away you go …

- **Imagine** having your very own professional e-commerce website with over 75 content-rich, search engine friendly pages that contain all of your own affiliate links for the bestselling products on the internet from 20 of the most respected and highest paying affiliate programs …

- **Imagine** that your new website comes with a subscription form that captures each visitor's name and email address – then automatically adds them to your own auto-responder that has been setup and pre-loaded with a complete 365-day email marketing campaign that promotes your website and top affiliate products on auto-pilot 24 hours a day, 7 days a week, 365 days a year ...

- **Imagine** that this entire website takes you less than 15 minutes to build simply by pressing a few buttons inside innovative *Plug-In Profit MEGA Site*™ software program that you can download right now ...

You can have it all now – and you can have it all for free. All you have to do is pay for the hosting and even that comes at substantially discounted cost. For complete details on this unique deal visit this website: www.PlugInProfitSite.com.

Now this is what I call a niche opportunity.

13
Why niche marketing
works best

There isn't a successful online marketer anywhere in the world who would dispute the assertion that niche is the only way to go: niche markets, niche customers, niche produce. And this applies whether you create your own produce or opt for someone else's to promote.

- Identify your niche market.

- Identify your niche customers.

- Identify the produce the niche market and its customers want.

WHY THE MAJOR DOT COMS BOMBED

The cardinal sin the major players were guilty of in the spectacular crash of a few years back was that they all set out to sell everything to everyone; everything they thought that everyone *needed*. Their profligacy cost them and their backers millions upon millions of pounds. It cost them dearly because they considered niche markets too small, too insignificant, too expensive to reach, and too slow to develop in the reckless drive for immediate returns to match their massive investment. They were wrong every which way; they paid the price: they bombed.

WHY MOST ONLINE BUSINESSES FAIL BEFORE THEY BEGIN

It's sad, but even today the vast majority of online businesses still manage to fail before they actually begin.

'Why?' you ask.

Because 98 per cent of the people *trying* to do business online, don't know how to go about choosing a niche.

In fact, most of them make one of two huge mistakes:

- Mistake No. 1 – **Targeting a market that is too broad**: e.g. trying to compete with Amazon.com by selling books or other common household items online.

- Mistake No. 2 – **Targeting a niche that is overly saturated**: e.g. trying to get a foothold in the 'Internet Marketing' or 'How To Make Money Online' niche.

WHAT IS IT THAT PEOPLE WANT MOST FROM THE INTERNET?

This table of the top five e-commerce niche categories says it all:

Product	Buyers (millions)
Computers	4.3
Electronics	7.4
Software	9.6
CDs/Videos/DVDs	11.2
Digitised Books and Information	**17.5**

Source: Forrester Survey, 2004.

Information products outstrip all other e-commerce niche purchasing options and this opens the door to you in the development of your retirement money-maker plan.

The secret to success

The secret to long-term success online is to find tiny – but popular – niche markets that have little or no direct competition, and then create and sell digitised information products to these niches.

When people go online to buy, they buy what they *want*

That's it then in a nutshell. When people go online to buy, they buy what they *want*; not what they necessarily *need* or what other people say is good for them. Allow me to illustrate with a true story that dates back long before we had colour television, mobile phones, or the internet.

HOW NICHE NOUS SPAWNED A 50-YEAR CAREER FOR JOE LOSS

The famous bandleader Joe Loss was a master at finding out what his niche customers wanted and as a result stayed at the top of his profession for over 50 years. When Joe and his orchestra played in provincial dance halls he invariably used his break time for market research. While the band members sloped off for a beer, Joe mingled with the patrons enquiring after their current tastes in popular music. He did so because he never took for granted that what was hip today would necessarily be so tomorrow. Joe always had his finger on the pulse of cyclical change and frequently bucked the trends that other bandleaders followed unremittingly in the mistaken belief that they knew which musical styles dancers *needed*.

How do I know this? I'll tell you. As a young man in my early twenties I frequented these same provincial dance halls and I was privileged to be selected as one of Joe's interviewees, not once, but twice. On the second occasion I asked Joe why he was so interested in my melodic preferences – and he told me why.

Joe knew his niche market inside out, knew his customers, and always knew how to give them exactly what they wanted. He knew because he *asked* them and so too can you ask your customers, not face to face, but virtually – as you will discover as we continue.

HOW TO IDENTIFY AN EASY-TO-TARGET NICHE MARKET

Don't treat the following questions lightly; think seriously about them and go beyond the obvious. Many opportunities and breakthroughs lie in the final stretch. In other words, expand your mind, because the best ideas will probably be found further down the list past the first more obvious ones. Just jot down your ideas no matter how silly or implausible. You will never know until you test.

Come up with a list of at least 100 ideas by answering these questions:

- What you enjoy doing?
- What do you do voluntarily?
- What are your hobbies or special interests?
- What do you do (assuming you are just approaching retirement) when you are not working?
- What did you love to do when you were much younger?
- What do you do really well?
- What do you do *not so well* but still enjoy?
- What skills and knowledge have you accumulated from your working life?
- In which areas do people ask for your help?
- Compile a list of the occupations you were involved in down the years. Now list the things you liked about each job; list the things you know about each job; list the things you reckon you excelled at while you worked in each job; list the things you hated and why.
- What schools did you attend?
- What courses did you take? In which subjects did you do well? Did friends ask for your help; if so, in which subjects?
- In which sports did you participate?

- Where have you travelled to? Why? For what purposes? What did you learn? Who did you meet?

- Make a list of your friends. What do *they* like to do? In which areas are they expert? Would they be interested in joining you in a niche venture?

At this point you should have a list of 100 ideas. If not, keep adding to the list until you do. Admittedly, this exercise may take more than a day to accomplish but force your mind to go beyond the obvious. Look closer and dig deeper but if you are stuck and need more ideas, try these alternative routes:

1. Visit your favourite bookstore; browse over the 10 best-selling non-fiction books.

2. Visit your favourite book aisles; which books rouse your curiosity?

3. Visit your favourite newsstand; which newspapers or magazines interest you? Which ones do you read? Which ones do you buy?

4. Ask around, friends and relatives in particular. 'In what things do you think I am most interested? What things do you think I do well? About which topics do I talk most?' (Some of the answers may surprise you.)

After you're done, narrow your list down to three to five topics that appeal most to you; topics that tickle your fancy This is important because you have to like the idea and show much more than just a passing interest in the topic. If you create a potentially profitable retirement pursuit around this topic, you may be working at it for years and have fun doing it. So choose something that you enjoy, that you like, that *fascinates* you.

Now take the core words from your narrowed-down list of ideas, and type them into a few major search engines; investigate each item on your list.

- Do you see a pattern emerging?
- Can you find websites, newsgroups and newsletters that focus on that very interest?
- *Do your interests coincide with a niche market?*
- How large and identifiable is the niche?
- Who is the competition?
- What do they do?
- What are they selling?
- What are their target markets?
- How are they positioned?
- What's missing?
- What problem can you perceive that is not being currently addressed?
- Could you provide a solution?
- Could you conceive a product or service that the niche wants and will buy?

To achieve this latter objective, frequent the newsgroups, forums, and discussion groups related to your niche. Look at the questions being posted daily. Talk to the participants. Ask questions. This is how to determine what potential niche customers *want*, not necessarily *need*.

HOW TO FIND A PRODUCT OR SERVICE THAT PEOPLE WANT

By now you should have identified one or two easy-to-target markets and if you have done your research properly you have probably also identified a problem the target market is currently experiencing. If you haven't found one yet, keep looking. It may take a little more time. If people are asking questions on newsgroups, forums, discussion groups that you do not understand, contact them individually and request clarification. Keep going until you uncover a problem, a want, a need.

Now brainstorm again.

- What types of produce or service can you develop, locate or resell to help solve the identified problem?

- More importantly, determine whether your solution will sell.

Once you have defined a product or service, ascertain if your identified niche market is willing to part with hard cash to own your prescribed solution. Always remember, a recognised 'want' does not necessarily translate into sales. Just because someone apparently wants something it does not mean that they will want it badly enough to splash out cash. If your target audience is unwilling to purchase your product or service for whatever reason, or if you have identified more problems than you can solve, discard the market and move on to the next one. Never get hung up on trying to flog a dead horse.

Nonetheless, the most profitable products are those you can develop yourself because that way you control the costs. But you may have neither the skills nor the resources to achieve this. If that is the case, look around for a joint partner who already *has the solution* but is not doing a very good job of marketing it. Make an offer – and be sure to put it in writing. You'll never know if you don't ask.

Throughout the entire process of finding a product or service that people want, bear in mind that while almost anything sells over the internet, you should focus on produce that can be digitised and easily automated. Become 'auto-pilot'-minded. This will allow you to expand into several profitable online retirement pursuits that combine to create multiple income streams.

Above all – think niche.

TESTING THE POTENTIAL FOR YOUR NICHE MARKET

You might well ask, 'How do I go about testing the market?' You will begin by using the search engines to gauge the popularity of keywords and key phrases related to your particular niche. The number of sites displayed for, say, the keyword 'golf swing' will provide a notional indication of the overall niche market size. But that is not enough. Now you need to establish how many times per month 'golf swing' is being searched for by users. When you've determined that you can also determine the keyword's popularity, that is the number of times the term is searched for as opposed to sites available for scrutiny.

Are there more sites than users searching for the keyword? If there are, you've just found an oversaturated niche, so drop it.

Are there more users than sites available for searching? Then you've located an under-worked niche, so go for it.

AN EXCEPTIONAL TOOL THAT PROVIDES THE ANSWERS

Here is an exceptional tool that will provide the answers in relation to every niche keyword you can come up with.

Good Keywords – Measures everything from keyword popularity to a website's popularity and beyond. Download the software at this site: www.goodkeywords.com.

You've located the perfect keyword(s) for your perfect niche but now you want to find out more about your market.

Here's what to do. Go to www.google.com and undertake a search for 'niche articles' (replacing the word 'niche' with the root word relating to your niche). You will be presented with hundreds (if not thousands) of highly informative free articles.

HOW TO KNOW IF YOU'VE STRUCK IT NICHE

- You have located an easy-to-target niche market.
- It is easy for you and other people to identify.

- You know where to reach your perfect customers.

- There are sufficient numbers of them.

- There are newsgroups they frequent.

- There are websites they visit.

- There are newsletters they subscribe to.

- You have identified a problem this niche market is currently experiencing.

- You have developed a product or service to provide a solution.

- It's something your potential niche customers *want*, not need.

- You have tested the market and now know they will buy from you.

HOW TO DEVELOP A GREAT SALES PROCESS

The next step in the formula is arguably the most challenging. The difficulty lies not in the principle but in its application; knowing what works in online promotion and what does not. So vital is this challenge that the remainder of the book is devoted to its exposition.

- Finding a great website name.

- Registering your website address as your trading name.

- Developing a compelling sales message.

- Obtaining the required e-commerce services.

- Developing systems for the fulfilment of your orders.

- Developing sound customer service strategies.

- Capturing visitor names and email addresses.

- Remaining in contact with both customers and website visitors.

- Designing, optimising, uploading your website.

- Developing strategies to attract online buyers …

  - search engines

- newsletters
- classified ads
- banner ads
- affiliate reselling
- article submissions
- linking strategies
- web page content
- online publicity
- offline publicity.

SECRETS TO UNLOCKING ESSENTIAL CORE NICHE FACTORS

Fig. 8. *Niche Factors*: a special report.

You will find them all in *Niche Factors*: a special report that costs $27 (approx. £15) – I use it all the time and to me it is worth ten times what I paid for it. But you can have it for free by sending a blank email to jimgreen@writing-for-profit.com with 'NICHE FACTORS' in the subject box.

Now let's move on to the vital matter of publicising your product because if you are not prepared to learn how to promote effectively you might as well stop reading right now.

KEY FACTORS THAT COMBINE TO GUARANTEE EFFECTIVE PROMOTION

14

How to promote your produce online

You have arrived at the halfway stage in the formulation of your retirement money-maker plan.

- You have examined a myriad of opportunities, offline and online, and hopefully like me have come to the conclusion that online is the faster, easier, less stressful route to take.

- You also know that attempting to sell everything to everyone is a complete waste of time and that niche is the only way to go.

Now you must learn how to promote your produce online because without mastering the essential elements, your profitable retirement recreation will rapidly develop into a pointless pursuit. It will be like slavering for hours on end over an exotic menu for the world's most expansive and imaginative banquet but forgoing the delights because you haven't taken the trouble to learn how to place an order.

The rest of this book focuses exclusively on the key factors that combine to guarantee effective promotion. There is nothing difficult about any of them; it is simply a matter of comprehension and application.

FOURTEEN KEY FACTORS THAT COMBINE TO GUARANTEE EFFECTIVE ONLINE PROMOTION

1. Choosing your domain name.
2. Building a website to generate sales.

3. Creating interesting content.

4. Devising powerful keywords.

5. Using 'smart' pages.

6. Attracting traffic to your site.

7. Test-marketing before you press the button.

8. Using e-books to promote and sell your produce.

9. Writing articles to lure visitors.

10. Linking to other websites.

11. Email marketing.

12. Creating your own newsletter.

13. Building a list of prospects.

14. Accepting credit cards and online cheques.

Choosing your domain name

Getting the domain name right, right at the start, is germane to the success of your profitable online retirement pursuit. It is your cyberspace calling card and to work effectively in all matters of promotion it should reflect your niche market and your niche produce. (Chapter 15)

Building a website to generate sales

You have a choice of approach: one-page or multi-dimensional. Some propositions require only a single page to generate sales; others of a more complex nature may call for up to 20 pages to get the message across. (Chapter 16)

Creating interesting content

Regardless of the approach, your web page(s) must be content-rich if they are to attract the attention of the search engine 'spiders' and achieve top ranking status, featuring in positions between 1–30. Content-rich pages are also vital to hold the attention of your website visitors and persuade them to make a purchase. (Chapter 17)

Devising powerful keywords

Rich content alone won't always cut the mustard. You must also learn how to lace it with powerful keywords and key phrases. (Chapter 18)

Using 'smart' pages

You can use the smart page technique to supplement overall promotion and you can do it whether you opt for a one-page website or the multi-dimensional approach. (Chapter 19)

Attracting traffic to your site

Attracting website traffic is a science all on its own and even if you decide to put it all on automatic pilot you must still learn the basics to make it work. (Chapter 20)

Test-marketing before you press the button

You've found the perfect niche market, identified a problem it is currently experiencing, know how to reach your potential customers, and are confident you can provide a solution for what they appear to want most. Now what? You must test out your idea before you press the button on full-scale promotion. (Chapter 22)

Using e-books to promote and sell your produce

Your solution will almost certainly take the shape of a digitised product, software or service. That is what you will be selling. But you can also use the concept to promote your niche produce. (Chapter 23)

Writing articles to lure visitors

Many experienced online practitioners (me included) will tell you that submitting articles to core sites and directories is a powerful way to attract regular streams of visitors to your website. Learn how and where to submit. (Chapter 24)

Linking to other websites

All of the major search engines will reward you with higher positioning when you have multiple links to other *related* websites. Learn what to do to achieve this – and what not to do. (Chapter 25). Combine article submission with linking and the results can prove spectacular.

Email marketing

Once the linchpin of online promotion, email marketing has taken a nosedive in popularity due entirely to the mindless antics of irresponsible spammers. You can still use the technique but only when you know how to adhere to the new regulations. (Chapter 26)

Creating your own newsletter

Selling something new to someone who has already bought from you is 100 times easier than finding new customers. Don't leave money lying on the table. Learn to communicate regularly with your existing customers. That way you will attract new ones much more easily. (Chapter 27)

Building a list of prospects

This is the major add-on benefit developing out of the creation of your own newsletter. But there are other ways. (Chapter 28)

Accepting credit cards and online cheques

Without this facility your profitable retirement pursuit will rapidly develop into a non-profit-making hobby. Learn how to do it without investing in merchant status. (Chapter 30)

EIGHT MORE BUILDING BLOCKS TO ATTRACT CUSTOMERS

To round off this introduction to online promotion the following article by an American lady Julie Chance – www.strategies-by-design.com/ – provides you with another eight building blocks to ensure success for your produce.

> Whether you are a Fortune 500 company or a one person shop, to be successful, you must have a plan to attract customers and you must implement it consistently. However, it doesn't have to cost a fortune and you don't have to be a creative genius.
>
> The key to attracting customers is developing a marketing strategy that forms a solid foundation for your promotional efforts. Implementing promotional activities such as advertising, direct mail or even networking and one-to-one sales efforts without a marketing plan is like buying curtains for a house you're building before you have an architectural plan. How would you even know how many curtains to buy or what size they needed to be?
>
> To develop a strong marketing foundation here is what to do:
>
> ## 1. Define your product or service:
>
> - How is your virtual product or service packaged?
> - What is it that your customers are really buying?
>
> You may be selling web-based software tools but your clients are buying increased productivity, improved efficiency and cost savings.

- What problem does your service solve?

- What need does your product meet?

- What want does it fulfil?

2. Identify your ideal customer:

Everyone or anybody might be potential clients for your product. However, you probably don't have the time or money to market to everyone or anybody.

- Who is your ideal customer?

- Who does it make sense for you to spend your time and money promoting your service to?

You might define your ideal customer in terms of income, age, geographic area, number of employees, revenues, industry, etc. For example a massage therapist might decide her target market is women with household incomes of $75,000 or more who live in the uptown area.

3. Differentiate yourself from the competition:

Even if there are no direct competitors for your service, there is always competition of some kind. Something besides your product is competing for the potential client's money.

- What is it and why should the potential customer spend his or her money with you instead?

- What is your competitive advantage or unique selling proposition?

4. Find a niche:

- Is there a customer group that is not currently being served or is not being served well?

- Are there customer wants that are not being met?

A niche strategy allows you to focus your marketing efforts and dominate your market, even if you are a small player.

5. Develop awareness:

It is difficult for a potential client to buy your product or service if they don't even know or remember it exists.

- Generally a potential customer will have to be exposed to your product five to 15 times before they are likely to think of your product when the need arises;

- Needs often arise unexpectedly; you must stay in front of your clients consistently if they are going to remember your product when that need arises.

6. Build credibility:

Not only must clients be aware of your product or service, they also must have a positive disposition toward it.

- Potential customers must trust that you will deliver what you say you will;

- With large or risky purchases, you need to give them the opportunity to 'sample', 'touch', or 'taste' the product in some way.

For example, a trainer might gain credibility and allow potential customers to sample their product by offering free, hour long presentations on topics related to their area of specialty.

7. Be consistent:

Be consistent in every way and in everything you do. This includes the look of your collateral materials, the message you deliver, the level of customer service, and the quality of the product. Being consistent is more important than having the best product. This in part is the reason for the success of chains. Whether you're going to Little Rock, Arkansas or New York City, if you reserve a room at a Courtyard Marriott you know exactly what you're going to get.

8. Maintain focus:

Focus allows for more effective utilisation of the scarce resources of time and money. Your promotional budget will bring you greater return if you use it to promote a single product to a narrowly defined group of customers and if you promote that same product to that same customer group over a continuous period of time. Before you develop a virtual brochure, run an ad, implement an email campaign, join an organisation for networking or even conduct a sales call, ask yourself this question, 'Do I really know who my ideal customers are and not only what they need but also what they *want*?' If you can't honestly answer yes to this question, your promotional strategy may be built on a foundation of sand.

Wise words from a highly successful online promoter.

15
Why choosing your own domain name is essential

A question that I frequently hear is 'Do I really need to have my own domain name?' The one word answer is 'Yes'. If you put up your site with one of the free web hosting services, the one that benefits most is the hosting company. The last person to benefit is you. There are a number of reasons why having your own domain name is a must for your profitable retirement pursuit:

THE IMPORTANCE OF HAVING YOUR OWN DOMAIN NAME

1. When you have your own domain name, the address of your website will be of the form www.yourcompany.com. On the other hand, if you put up your site on one of the free servers, the address of your website will be something like www.somefreewebsite.com/yourtradingname.

   - Which of these sounds more professional?

   - Which of these is easier to remember?

   I leave you to make your own judgement.

2. The way to make money online is to build up credibility among your customers. Having your own domain name is the first step in doing that. Your customers will feel more comfortable buying whatever it is that you are selling if you have your own domain name. They get an immediate impression that they are dealing with a credible concern rather than with some fly-by-night operator.

3. When you have your own domain name, you can have multiple email aliases of the form alias@yourcompany.com. This allows you to assign different email aliases to different functions, all of them pointing to your actual email address.

   - For questions related to the products and services that you sell, you can have an email address like sales@yourcompany.com.

   - For questions related to the newsletter that you publish, you can have an email address like editor@yourcompany.com.

   - For comments/suggestions about your website, you can direct your customers to feedback@yourcompany.com or webmaster@yourcompany.com.

   Having different email addresses for different functions not only makes it easier for you to filter email using your email client programme but also gives your customers the impression that yours is an established company with whom it is safe to do business.

4. Many search engines give serious emphasis to the home page of a particular domain, i.e. other things remaining the same, a home page of a domain will often rank higher for a particular keyword than any other page. When you use some of the free hosting services your index.html page is the home page of your site but not of that domain. Hence in these search engines your site will find it very difficult to make it to the top 20 or top 30 let alone the top 10 for some of the really competitive keywords. Just think of the amount of traffic that you will lose if this happens.

5. Some search engines are now refusing to 'spider' websites which are hosted by the free web services. For instance, if you have a freely hosted site you would, until recently have got the infamous error message saying that too many pages have been submitted if you tried to submit your site to AltaVista. And now while Altavista reports 'your URL has been submitted for processing', don't be fooled. If you try to submit rest assured that AltaVista will not spider your pages even though it says that your site has

been accepted for submission. Can you afford that?

6. When your site is hosted by some of the free web hosts you will find it very difficult to get it listed in major directories like Yahoo!, The Open Directory or Zeal. Although Yahoo will never admit that it won't add a commercial site which is hosted by one of the free web hosts, in practice, it will be a miracle if you can get your site listed. Listing is difficult enough even when you have your own domain. Don't make your task more difficult than it needs to be.

The small fee that you pay per year for your own domain name is loose change compared to the benefits that you accrue. You can check out the availability of domain names and register new domains at www.whois.com.

HOW TO CHOOSE DOMAIN NAMES

So, now that you are convinced that you need your own domain, how should you name it? Here are a few dos and don'ts. While the availability of domains which follow all of these rules may have become limited, try to follow as many as possible.

1 – Consider naming your company and registering a domain name starting with the digit 1.

Better still choose a name starting with '1st'. Why? When people create directories of websites they have to decide how they are going to classify the submissions. One way to classify sites is to list them on the basis of how 'good' they are. Another way is to simply list them in chronological order (and sometimes in reverse chronological order) based on the dates the sites were submitted.

The other and far more popular classification system is alphabetic. Now, the first character in the ASCII chart which can be used as the first character in a domain name is the digit 0. The next character is the digit 1. Normally, you wouldn't want to start a domain name with the digit 0 since it might send out all the wrong signals to your customers. Instead name your domains starting with the digit 1. More specifically, name your domains starting with '1st' (for example 1st-creative-writing-course.com). This will ensure that you get a high alphabetical placement in those directories which classify sites alphabetically. Furthermore, depending on the niche market in which your retirement pursuit operates it may also send the right message across to your customers – it indicates that you are the first venture to consider in the niche.

And guess what – the mother of all directories – Yahoo! – lists websites alphabetically based on the *title* that had been submitted. Yahoo wants the title to be the official name of the site. This implies that sites which start with the digit 1 will be placed at or near the top of a category. That's why 1st-creative-writing-course.com features in the Top 10 on Yahoo! out of 8,000,000+ competitive sites. Assuming that you can get your site listed in Yahoo! just consider what a top ranking in one of the categories in the directory can do for its popularity.

Furthermore, a small caveat here. If you are going to name a domain starting with '1st', also register the domain which starts with 'ist'. Then, have the domain containing the vowel 'i' redirect visitors to the domain containing the digit 1. This is because people will often type in 'ist' when they mean '1st' and vice-versa. Also, for every email alias that you create for the domain containing '1st' (like sales@1stcompany.com), you should create the corresponding email alias for the domain containing 'ist' (like sales@istcompany.com). Incidentally, this strategy is especially significant in the case of registering a domain for a new venture.

2 – Don't want to start your domain name with '1st'?

Consider starting it with 'A', 'B' or 'C'. Although domains starting with A, B or C will be listed after those starting with the 10 digits, you can still get a pretty high alphabetical placement.

3 – Try to register a domain which contains a popular keyword applicable for your niche.

This will help your customers remember your domain name better. Furthermore, for searches conducted in Yahoo!, a higher ranking will be given to those websites which contain the keywords in the title. And according to Yahoo! instructions, the title should always be the official name of the site. Thus, if the domain name contains a keyword, you will be able to include the keyword in the title which will improve your ranking. As a minor side-benefit, this can also help to increase the ranking of your website in some search engines. Hence, in an ideal case, you should register a domain of the form 1st[keyword].com (without the brackets of course).

4 – Don't register a domain containing the digit 0.

Avoid zero unless it is going to be part of a recognisable word (like 1000 or 2000). This is because the digit 0 is often confused with the vowel O. If you feel that you must register a domain with the digit 0, make sure that you also register the corresponding domain containing the vowel O.

5 – Try to avoid using domains that contain '2' for 'To', '4' for 'For', 'u' for 'You'.

Your customers will easily get confused if you do this. However, if you must register such a domain, register the expanded form of the domain as well, e.g. if you are registering www.greatthings2do.com, also register www.greatthingstodo.com.

6 – Should you or should you not use hyphens in your domain?

Well, the jury is out on this question. While some internet marketers will tell you that domains containing hyphens are difficult to remember, spell and pronounce, others will state that they are, in fact, easy to remember, spell and pronounce. The controversy surrounding hyphens didn't bother me when I registered www.writing-for-profit.com. Personally, I would consider that whether or not hyphens are helpful has to be determined on a case by case basis. However, if you register a domain containing hyphens, make sure that you also register the corresponding domain without the hyphens. Once you do that, you can simply redirect visitors from the domain without the hyphens to the domain with the hyphens.

7 – Don't make your primary domain too long.

Even though 67 character domains are a reality, exactly how many of your users will want to type a domain name like www.thisisanexampleofaverylargedomainname.com?

8 – Always use '.com'.

Avoid using domains ending in 'nu' or 'to'. Your venture will have little credibility if you do. You can consider registering a '.net' domain, but since most people are more familiar with '.com', it is better to stick to convention.

While it is unlikely that you will be able to register a domain which satisfies all the rules that I outlined above, try to follow as many of them you can.

> **TIP**
>
> Visit www.1stSearchRanking.com where you can invest in their service promising top placement in all of the search engines or your money back. Alternatively, consider using either of the website hosting services featured in the next chapter. Both do it all for you automatically.

16
Mini- v. maxi-websites

There's a lot of be said in favour of both, but for niche markets and niche produce (which is where *you* ought to be focusing your profitable online retirement pursuit) it is best to opt for mini sites (a.k.a. one/two/three page websites). Read on and I'll give you several sound reasons why.

Maxi or multi-page sites on the other hand are more practical where you have lots of information to impart before you can interest prospects sufficiently to make a purchase or to instruct them where you are offering training services. I use both options where applicable and for the purposes just stated.

THE PERFECT VEHICLE FOR E-BOOKS AND SOFTWARE

The mini-site approach is perfect for niche produce such as stand-alone e-books and software because it provides a simple one-shot marketing vehicle: sales letter coupled with online order form. You will be almost certainly be starting out with a single product in your profitable retirement venture so a well constructed mini-site such as I am about to illustrate will suffice. Later, when you are up and running with several products you might well consider switching to the multi-dimensional approach.

Mini-sites will work for you providing you have:

* identified your niche market;
* know where your niche customers hang out;

- mastered the art of creating a compelling sales letter;
- learned how to build a one-shot marketing site;
- learned how to promote it effectively.

THE ADVERTORIAL NATURE OF THE MINI-SITE

The best and most successful mini-sites aren't designed as in-your-face billboard advertisements. Certainly they are sales letters but presented in a format that resembles the advertorial style we are all familiar with as we browse through our daily newspapers. They are informative and more often than not, touchy-feely. They set up the stall, identify a problem or highlight a want, promise a solution, make a spiel, elaborate on the benefits, and wind up with a pitch for the sale.

This approach isn't new; it has been worked successfully for over 200 years.

Recall just a few years back when hardly a week went by without at least one 4/6/8-page promotional piece in the shape of a sales letter popping through your letterbox. Mini-sites are the virtual equivalent.

CREATING THE BASIC COMPONENTS FOR YOUR SALES LETTER

The header graphic block

This is an illustrative visual that announces the title of the produce. It works best when there is a hint of colour and it could contain a picture. It can also be a generic block covering multiple produce such as one I use myself: *Retirement MoneyMakers*.

The headline promise

Comprises a few pithy words that highlight the major benefit you are offering: the solution to an identified problem.

The testimonials/credential block

Here is where you lay out your credentials for creating the product, and reproduce one or two testimonials. You won't have any from paying customers yet, but what you do instead is pass the product around friends and colleagues to elicit some glowing reviews.

The product introduction block

Introduce your proposition as the solution to a given problem and include a graphic in the shape of a digitally generated e-book cover (see Chapter 23 for the ideal software).

The benefits block

Bullet-point all of the produce benefits (not the features). This will more readily assist readers to visualise how the problem will vanish when they own the product.

The guarantee block

Don't be shy about offering a watertight guarantee. This is how to convert procrastinators and stave off refund requests.

The call-to-action summary block

Make it positive, make it compelling, make it bullish; make it easy to buy, make your prospects reach out for their credit cards.

Visit www.1st-creative-writing-course.com to view an example of how to lay out the ideal mini-website sales letter.

ACCESSING ALL-IN-ONE SOLUTION SOFTWARE

Here is the best tool on the market for constructing mini-sites. It does everything automatically to ensure that your site is winner.

- Designs the header block.

- Writes the sales letter (yes, you read correctly, it *actually* writes your pitch). Follow the promptings of the software, answer a few questions, follow the directions, and watch your sales letter take shape.

- Creates the mini-site *per se*.

This amazing all-in-one software costs $97 (approx. £54) and is available for download at www.saleslettergenerator.com.

THE PERFECT HOSTING SERVICE FOR YOUR MINI-SITES

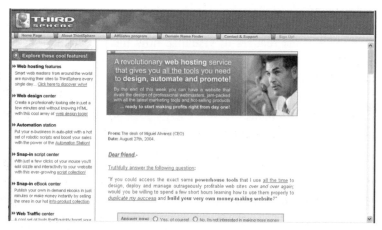

Fig. 9. The perfect hosting service for mini-sites.

With the Third Sphere hosting service you get:

1. Choice of fonts.

2. Context-sensitive menus when building.

3. Common Gateway Interface (CGI) bin.

4. CGI scripts library.

5. Uploading to server.

6. Password protected pages.

7. Custom error pages.

8. Back-up system.

9. Source code editing.

10. Spell check.

11. Spam blockers.

12. Total Marketing automation.

13. Traffic centre and tools.

14. Upload files *without* File Transfer Protocol (FTP).

15. Edit HTML on screen.

16. Anti-virus software.

17. Secure space (product delivery).

18. PDF e-book creator (from Word files).

Plus, perhaps most important of all, it provides you with the ability to create and market *unlimited numbers of mini-sites* with separate directories but all under the *same* domain. What a saving. It works like this: you register a niche domain name, say, howtoproducts-xl.com. Using Third Sphere hosting here's what you can do.

Create a sub-domain attached to the main site, for example www.articles.howtoproducts-xl.com and continue for as many separate associated e-products as you like. I use this service myself and consider it a bargain at $25 (approx. £13.90) per month.

thirdspherehosting.com/plus/?xstcreat&id=xstcreat&pkg=

HOW A SINGLE MINI-SITE CAN SPAWN THOUSANDS MORE

Following hard on the heels of what I've just said, think about this; with the investment of around £5 or so for a single niche domain and the Third Sphere hosting service you could proceed from the original mini-site to dozens, hundreds or even thousands more with each promoting an individual product.

Here is how you do it ...

In Chapter 2 you learned how to brainstorm your accumulated intelligence on a favourite topic and position it in such a format as to provide the substance for a book. Now look again at your notes and regard them this time as the linchpin that gives you the subject matter for your very first digitised information product.

- Create the information product (you will learn how in Chapter 23).

- Create your first mini-site.

- Use Third Sphere as the hosting service.

Now look again at your notes and compare them with the chapters in your information product. You will find enough meat there to:

- create a second information product out of one of the chapters, then another, and another, and so on until you have exhausted the topic;

- create as many more mini-sites as you have information products.

Now reflect, you have done all this from one original topic and one mini-site, but you don't have to stop there. There are many other topics you know a great deal about, and what you don't know you can always research.

Now set about repeating the exercise detailed above for a variety of other topics. Register domains, create the information produce and build the mini-sites. This is horizontal and vertical expansion at its most profitable, creating multiple streams of residual income.

You'd like proof to confirm what I'm claiming?

Try this ... and bear in mind I've only just started using the Third Sphere service:

From the advent of 1st-creative-writing-course.com and its ensuing popularity I developed another three sibling mini-sites as follows ...

1. 1st-creative-writing-course.com/makemoney.html

2. 1st-creative-writing-course.com/gettingpublished.html

3. 1st-creative-writing-course.com/wfp.html

But I didn't stop there ...

I proceeded to invest in more £5 domains, beginning with:

4. retirement-moneymakers.com

5. start-a-business-masterplan.com

The fifth domain spawned four more siblings, all promoting related produce.

6. start-a-business-masterplan.com/

7. 1st-creative-writing-course.com/homeshopoffice/online.html

8. 1st-creative-writing-course.com/mistakes/acm.html

9. 1st-creative-writing-course.com/progress/pro.html

Then guess what?

I set up howtoproducts-xl.com to house and horizontally promote all my websites.

And then to drive traffic to this main portal site – and all of its clients – I created howtoproducts-xl.com/articles.html

What does it contain?

Links to 20 more individual sibling mini-sites; each one featuring a specific, highly targeted article directed at attracting prospects to one or more of products contained in websites 1–11.

1. howtoproducts-xl.com/article1.html

2. howtoproducts-xl.com/article2.html

3. howtoproducts-xl.com/article3.html

4. howtoproducts-xl.com/article4.html

5. howtoproducts-xl.com/article5.html

6. howtoproducts-xl.com/article6.html

7. howtoproducts-xl.com/article7.html

8. howtoproducts-xl.com/article8.html

9. howtoproducts-xl.com/article9.html

10. howtoproducts-xl.com/article10.html

11. howtoproducts-xl.com/article11.html

12. howtoproducts-xl.com/article12.html

13. howtoproducts-xl.com/article13.html

14. howtoproducts-xl.com/article14.html

15. howtoproducts-xl.com/article15.html

16. howtoproducts-xl.com/article16.html

17. howtoproducts-xl.com/article17.html

18. howtoproducts-xl.com/article18.html

19. howtoproducts-xl.com/article19.html

20. howtoproducts-xl.com/article20.html

So what have we achieved out of one single small monthly hosting fee?

- 32 revenue-producing websites at no cost other than that incurred for registering additional domain names.

Not a bad return for £20 …

thirdspherehosting.com/plus/?xstcreat&id=xstcreat&pkg=

WHEN YOU NEED TO USE THE MULTI-PAGE APPROACH

At the risk of boring you I refer yet again to www.writing-for-profit.com (Figure 1). This website uses the multi-dimensional approach because it has many functions to perform. It markets a comprehensive tutorial on the topic of writing niche non-fiction; it dispenses free e-books and complimentary reports on the subject; it provides instruction on e-writing; it contains a massive resources directory; it test markets disparate digitised produce, etc. And it also gives away completely free of charge reams of valuable information.

Why does it do all this?

Not to sell the tutorial; that's incidental. It does it all to sell more of my published hard copy titles in worldwide bookstores and online at Amazon.com.

That is why I use the multi-dimensional approach. You will have another reason when you come to consider it; multiple produce.

WHERE TO FIND THE IDEAL SOLUTION

If you were to forever manually operate all of the mandatory chores we will be discussing in future chapters you'd drive yourself nuts and, what's more, have no time left over to accomplish what you really set out to achieve: develop your own profitable retirement pursuit. Fortunately, that need not be the case. You have at your disposal a cutting edge tool to do it all for you automatically when you operate a multi-page website – but not before you've cut your teeth on the basics of manual operation. Why? Because only when you know 'how' can you appreciate 'why'.

The *Site Build It!* way to create and manage a multi-page website

What you need to make the most of the e-commerce experience is composite software that frees up time to enable you to concentrate on the primary function: marketing your retirement venture. Such all-embracing software is available to you and it is proving a popular route with many retiree entrepreneurs because it is less demanding and permits one-to-one virtual interfacing with potential customers.

Should this be of interest to you (and it's worth investigating) you might consider investing in the all-in-one tool that I use. It will set you back $499 (approx. £277) annually, but what you receive for your money is awesome. *Site Build It!* is available for immediate download at buildit.sitesell.com/interactive1.html.

Fig. 10. The ideal hosting service for multi-page sites.

Here is what you get for your investment

1. Domain name registration.
2. Hosting.
3. Power keyword research, analysis and implementation.
4. Graphic tools.
5. Point and Click page building.
6. Choice of page templates.
7. FTP to upload your files to server.
8. Form builder/Auto-responder.
9. Data transfer.

10. Email.

11. Newsletter publishing facility.

12. Brainstorming and researching for the right keywords.

13. Spam check.

14. Daily traffic stats and click analysis.

15. Search engine optimisation.

16. Automatic search engine submission.

17. Automatic search engine tracking.

18. Automatic search engine ranking.

19. Pay-per-click research and mass-bidding.

20. Four individual traffic headquarters.

21. Action guide and fast track guide.

22. Integrated online help.

23. Express ezine to keep you up to date on new developments.

24. Tips and techniques.

25. Customer support.

26. Facility for uploading/downloading digitised data.

The *Site Build It!* Traffic Centre outstrips by far all other alternatives I have so far encountered. Once you have the hang of it (and that doesn't take long) you just sit back, leave it all to the software as you watch your traffic soar day by day.

It's awesome!

HOW DESIGNING A 'HELPFUL' SITE CAN KILL PRODUCT SALES

If you need further proof of the respective merits of mini v. maxi websites read this convincing article by ace web designer Harold R. Fann.

Think you need an 'interesting' website with lots of valuable content, interactivity, and frequent updates to keep visitors returning? Think again!

Enticing visitors with lots of free content and hoping for an impulse sale is a quick way to starve. Yet so many how-to publications and gurus tell you to design a full site with helpful, frequently-updated content for surfers; wrong.

Selling single products

If you are selling one or two products, you need a one-page mini-site for each. You need to focus visitors' attention on each product – and keep it there.

EXAMPLE

A writer put lots of wonderful, useful content up on his website which attracts lots of visitors. The problem: no sales. He's trying to sell newsletter subscriptions but nobody is buying.

And why should they? They get tons of content already from him for free on his site. (Guess his mother never told him nobody will buy a cow if they get the milk for free.)

What should he do? He has only two choices:

- Kill most of the content at the site. Make the site into a single-page compelling letter that would cause people to subscribe to his newsletter;

- Same as above, but the letter should sell signing up for a free e-letter. Then he could use the free e-letter to sell subscriptions to the paid newsletter.

Another example: my sister was selling a book 'written' by her cat. She had a wonderful website, full of pictures, funny content, a page of advice from site visitors to the cat, etc. The only problem: she was selling just 1 book a month.

When I had her change it to a single page mini-site, which did nothing but sell the book, her sales went up to 20–30 per month.

Selling multiple products

If you are selling lots of products you need a catalogue (maxi) site. Don't try to pretend you're an informational site. What visitors will want most is easy, clear navigation so they can quickly find exactly the products that would best suit them. And, they want a simple, reliable, and secure ordering setup.

If you also have physical sites (bricks & mortar), you may do even better with a site that does nothing but offer discount coupons ...

EXAMPLE

A bricks and mortar department store built a full, wonderful website with lots of info and helpful tips but they didn't see any increase in visitors to their stores. Then they ruthlessly axed most of the content on their site, shrinking it to some pages that mainly offered discount coupons for particular merchandise. The result: traffic increased dramatically at the physical store and at the website. Most importantly – their sales increased.

Thinking about designing your own website? Just remember that when people are searching for a product, that's what they want to see. Don't divert them with tips and hints and other copy that can make them forget what they wanted in the first place. They probably did a search to find your site. Give them a chance to buy what they were searching for – from you!

Harold R. Fann is the author of *Time-Sucking, Money-Wasting Dangers to Avoid When Designing Your Own Website*. You can download it for free by clicking on the small link at the top of this page: www.HelpForWebDesign.com.

17
Why keywords are central to successful promotion

Target the wrong keywords and all your efforts at developing that great niche idea will be in vain. Net result: you will lose out on your profitable retirement pursuit.

TARGET THE RIGHT KEYWORDS AND YOUR TRAFFIC SKYROCKETS

Think long and hard about which keywords people are likely to use to find you. Which words would *you* choose to search for your niche idea? Make lists of keywords and then combine them into two or three word phrases.

For example, you rarely want to target a *single* keyword because with the billions of words indexed on the web right now; one keyword won't normally cut it on the average search. People learn quickly that if they type in 'properties' they get listings for property from all over the world. It would be nice if your URL popped up there on those extremely broad keywords – but a better use of your time is to *pair* the generic keyword with something more specific. You might get lucky and rank well on just 'properties' as it is in your page – but if not, you'll probably end up at somewhere like 2035 (or worse) in 'UK properties'.

Using *paired keywords* will also bring you far more qualified prospects for your product or service.

HOW PEOPLE CONDUCT KEYWORD SEARCHES

Statistically, most people search with two to three word phrases to avoid getting back too many unrelated matches. Keep this in mind when you design your page(s). Don't worry about there not being enough top ten slots where you can achieve a high ranking. True, there are some keywords that are very competitive, especially in the realm of work at home, shop or office opportunities. And if you find that no matter what you do, you can't get in that top ten spot for that word or phrase, just be creative. There are so many other keywords and keyword combinations where you can achieve a top ten ranking. It's really not very difficult at all. Once you tap into some phrases people are searching on to find your type of website, you'll have tapped into a continuous stream of *free advertising* for your business idea.

For example, if you don't achieve a good ranking on 'income idea', keep trying, but also be creative and target 'extra income idea' too. It's all about thinking like your customer or clientele – and finding a keyword combination that can *dominate* in the search engines. You'll often find that there are more people searching for these other phrases than were searching for the first phrase you thought of. In marketing, this is called carving out your niche, and when you work from home, isolating a unique niche in everything you do is germane to success.

If you're Microsoft, you can afford to fight over who has the best 'browser software'. But, for the rest of us, we know we can't always fight the big boys. So instead, do what savvy marketers do: detect a *niche* that few others are targeting and go after it.

Good management is the key to achieving a range of good rankings, each of which will bring you scores of new visitors – if you choose the proper keywords.

What are people searching for?

You need to know how many people are searching for one keyword over another keyword. 'Search volume' is the number of times a specific keyword is searched over a period of time. Having knowledge of search volumes will give you a sense of what is being searched for and what keywords you may want to focus on. A good place to look up search volumes is the suggestion tool at:

inventory.overture.com/d/searchinventory/suggestion/.

You will need to conduct market research to decide which keywords to focus on. Keep in mind that the more popular keywords are competing for the top listings – some are searched for several thousand times more than others. So the keywords you use to pull in users may vary accordingly. The goal is to find keywords or keyword phrases that get a good amount of searches but do not have as much competition.

More on this vital topic a few paragraphs on.

WHY TARGETING NICHE KEYWORDS BRINGS INSTANT RESULTS

Here is a practical illustration from my own experience when launching www.writing-for-profit.com. Targeting the correct keywords at the outset resulted in *839 top rankings* for my eighteen web pages within days of being 'spidered' by the major search engines. These are six of these keyword pairings and the initial rankings obtained on the very first day that listings were effected:

- Writing for profit – 6 x No. 1 Spots;
- Writing – 18 x No. 2 Spots;
- Extra income idea – 6 x No. 3 Spots;
- Extra income opportunity – 5 x No. 4 Spots;
- Residual income opportunity – 7 x No. 5 Spots;
- Residual income stream – 5 x No. 6 Spots.

Note the similarity of keyword pairings and the fact that the single keyword 'writing' broke the mould and scored highly. Note too that the first keyword phrase is also the URL for the website. Some claim that the composition of the website address makes little difference to the search engines but I disagree – and with good reason.

THE PROGRAM THAT HELPED GENERATE 839 TOP SPOTS

It's how you apply keyword power that determines success or failure in online marketing and you will discover why when you digest the content of *Site Build It!* It features a unique piece of software that takes the sting out of keyword selection, website construction, and the vitally important matter of traffic generation. Among the benefits is a manager program that takes your concept, submits it to rigorous testing and spews out a list of targeted keywords which is then further scrutinised for supply, demand – and profitability. Doing it this way you know where you stand with the search engines even before you submit!

> ### TIP
> Always use your own counsel in the final selection of power keywords. You know your own concept inside out (or at least, you should) so if you have an instinctive feeling about a certain key phrase of your own choosing and it doesn't come out top on profitability – retain it nevertheless. For example, 'writing for profit' rated well in the manager program analysis but it wasn't at number one – which it was in the search engine rankings we reviewed above.

HOW KEYWORDS IMPACT ON SALES

Because keyword power is the catalyst that directs visitors to your website it follows that attention to keyword selection is crucial if you are to attract sales for the end product of your retirement business idea. When people find you and your niche idea on the search engines they are invariably looking for something for nothing and if you provide them with freebies in the form of useful articles, tools, tips and techniques (but not too much or you'll give the store away) they will be all the more amenable to purchasing your product or service. They won't all rush to buy, so if sales are slow to begin with, take heart, you are on track with your niche idea. Persist and the flow of transactions will gradually increase.

Think about this: according to search engine statistics an average of *159,388 people* are searching on the internet *every day* for '*home business*' information.

Think too about this: many of these people will be among your visitors who will find you because they want to do what you do: *operate a home business*. In the light of this, it is sound practice to include two or more keywords aimed at these highly targeted prospects. They will be seeking free information on 'stay at home jobs', 'retirement business ideas', 'work at home ideas', 'work at home mums', 'work at home part time', 'work from home retirees' – and in particular, 'free work at home opportunities'. Give them what they want for free and a percentage of them will give you a sale for your home-based niche product or service.

FREE TOOLS TO ASSIST IN LOCATING POWERFUL KEYWORDS

Here are the tools I use in my own searches for powerful niche keywords and they come complete with easy-to-understand instructions. Basically, what you do is feed in a niche keyword and the software will not only tell you how many people have searched for the term during the previous four weeks but also provide a detailed list of similar keywords and a precise indication of their popularity.

You may download both tools free of charge.

- *Good keywords*: www.goodkeywords.com.
- *Wordtracker*: www.wordtracker.com.

So far so good, but irrespective of whether you opt for a mini or maxi website, powerful niche keywords will only work when your pages are content rich: the subject of the next chapter.

18

How to create content-rich pages for your website

You found your niche keywords using one or other of the prescribed tracking tools and now you must learn how to create content-rich pages judiciously interlaced with those sought after keywords. The principles apply equally whether you opt for the mini or maxi approach on website construction. You are already aware of the component text blocks that constitute the make-up of a mini-site and if multi-dimensional happens to be the route you prefer then you create an individual web page for each block, i.e. home page, product introduction, benefits, testimonials, credentials, guarantee, call to action, order, and so forth. (If you are unsure flip back to Chapter 16 for refreshment.)

WHY WORDS, NOT GRAPHICS, MAKE INTERESTING CONTENT

There is an old saying, 'a picture paints a thousand words'. Not so online. **Words rule, words are king.** Apart from your header and product blocks only add pictures and graphics if you are convinced they enhance and support your copy. That way you will see that most of the beautifully designed logos, banners and gizmos you had in mind will simply distract your readers from the one most important thing on your site – your sales message.

Now let's explore each task in turn ...

- Creating content rich pages.
- Interlacing them with keywords.

SO YOU RECKON THIS IS ALL NEW TO YOU?

Perhaps you're trying to write web copy for the first time. Perhaps you don't even consider yourself a writer at all. Perhaps you think it's too late to start now you are retired. Wrong. **You've been a creative writer all of your life**; when you were composing essays at school; when you were writing letters of application for new positions during your working life; when you put pen to paper to produce a reasoned argument why you had fallen behind in your council tax payments. You are an experienced writer but you don't give yourself credit for it.

This time you are charged with developing content for a topic you know a great deal about. You have researched it thoroughly, you have created a product around the topic (and even if you didn't create it yourself you have researched someone else's creation): you know more than you think you know.

You just follow some basic rules and let it all hang out. Don't get all strung up; have some fun instead.

SO WHAT'S SO DIFFERENT ABOUT WRITING WEB COPY?

There is no mystique. The techniques that work offline work equally well online. You have to make some changes of course to accommodate the restrictions imposed by the computer screen and the problems that navigation sometimes presents. But the successful techniques for effective web copy remain the same. And these techniques have been around for decades.

Good web copy doesn't attract the attention it deserves. Copy just isn't cool because well crafted persuasive text doesn't attract attention to itself. It just sits there on the page delivering its message skillfully and unobtrusively; focusing attention on the product and the reader; quietly doing its job of selling.

And most of the really successful internet marketers employ excellent, uncluttered copy on their sites. That's why they are successful.

It's so easy and cheap to build a website these days and set up a storefront. And that's great. There's room for you and your profitable retirement pursuit to compete alongside the big boys. And with no previous business or advertising experience you can build a 100-page super-duper animated site in minutes.

But when the sales don't come in, the answer seems to be to change the animated GIFs, Java scripts, site banners and other gizmos to grab the attention.

Meanwhile the clever marketers, the successful ones, rake in the sales with strong, professionally-crafted selling copy; copy they've taken the time to learn to write for themselves. They know it is words that sell, not gizmos. Which words?

Words that sell

After you have drawn up the approximate overall structure of your site, and before you design the fine details, decide *what* you're going to say and *who* you are going to say it to.

Now begin writing your copy

Write it, re-write it and cut out the dead wood. Crystallise your message. Hone it, polish it, and examine every single word for relevancy and maximum effect. Keep re-writing it until you're sure it's a winner. Don't be tempted to 'make do'. If it takes a week and it's still not right – spend another week until it is right. And a third week if need be until you're absolutely convinced you can't improve another single word. Remember, it is your profitable retirement pursuit that's at stake.

Here's an excellent tip

Print out your copy and read it out loud. If it doesn't sound like an everyday conversation there's something wrong. Have a friend read it out to you. If he/she stumbles over any words, or has to re-read a sentence, you'll know it needs re-writing.

Then build the website around your copy.

SEVENTEEN VITAL FACTORS POINTING THE WAY TO GOOD WEB WRITING

1. Far too many websites have no headline. If your web pages haven't got headlines, you will lose out. Just because readers are already at your page doesn't necessarily mean they know what to expect. A headline tells them what to expect. It also gives you, your offer, and your site an identity that is hopefully memorable.

2. Fire your biggest gun first – in your headline.

3. Push your USP into your reader's face.

4. Pack your message with **benefits**, benefits and more benefits.

5. Use plenty of white space.

6. Break your copy up into bite-sized chunks.

7. Make it easy to contact you from every page.

8. Place a 'Home' button on every page.

9. Make sure your copy is as long as it needs to be to get the entire message across.

10. Emphasise your key points.

11. Use testimonials with imagination. Don't just list them on a separate page. Your readers won't look for them.

12. Give the reader a call to action (for example, 'Order Now!').

13. Make it extremely easy to order.

14. Show your readers how to order.

15. At the ordering stage re-state your guarantee.

16. After they have submitted an order make sure they are told the

order has been received. Then send a 'Thank You' email. They need to be re-assured they have made the right decision. Prevent 'Buyer's Remorse', or they may cancel.

17. Be totally professional about absolutely everything.

ENCOURAGING INTERACTION WITH THE READER

Try always to persuade the reader to become involved in the message you are putting across and you can do this by:

1. connecting with readers immediately;
2. capturing their attention;
3. holding their interest;
4. speaking to their concerns;
5. answering their unasked questions;
6. overcoming objections;
7. compelling action;
8. valuing their time.

So there you have it. A very brief summary of the copywriting techniques used by the most successful marketers and copywriters on and off the web; just ordinary people with the good sense to stick to proven methods which achieve extraordinary results. Great interactive writing is easy to read, but often hard to write.

Here's a closing thought from a master of words, Winston Churchill: *'Had I had longer, it would have been shorter'*.

LACING THE TEXT WITH KEYWORDS TO ENTICE THE SPIDERS

It seems a shame to inflict your beautifully crafted web page copy with seemingly unrelated keywords and you may be tempted not to bother.

Resist the temptation. If you don't include them, your pages won't even be listed by the search engines let alone achieve top ranking positions. You see, while the spiders love rich content, they love judiciously sited keywords even more. Niche keywords are the bait that entices the spiders to rank your pages and position them accordingly – in the top spots.

However, be warned, do not overload your rich content with keywords; judicious placement is the operative term. Depending on the length of your page text, repeat your prime keyword three to five times; for the other keywords (you should use between six and eight) once or twice but no more.

The moral is …

• Content-rich pages with keywords get the top spots.

• Content-rich pages without keywords get ignored by the spiders.

19
Smart pages and
how to use them

Your profitable retirement pursuit is really beginning to shape up. From a niche concept you produced niche web copy and in turn created (preferably) a niche mini-website. Now, how would you like to see that handful of pages replicated dozens, hundreds, if not thousands of times over? You can do it if you adopt the 'smart' pages technique. You don't have to use it, you don't need to use it, but if you do you will be giving yourself many more bites at the cherry.

WHAT EXACTLY ARE 'SMART' PAGES?

Smart Pages are search-engine-optimised web pages that drive massive targeted traffic to your website. They are also known as gateway or doorway pages. The concept is revealed and fully explained in a refreshing new book *Under Oath* by Stephen Pierce (costs $47.97 and is available for download at www.the-whole-truth.com). It's worth having a look at the website because even if you if you don't buy the book you'll get additional information on the topic for free.

Over the years Stephen tested numerous methods of getting higher rankings in search engines, but without success. One day he developed some pages without any of the methods he had tried before and uploaded them to his site. Tired of not having success from his previous techniques he paid little attention to the exercise until he started getting a lot of sales and discovered that those specific 'smart' pages were getting top positions. Since then Stephen has refined the pages and currently has hundreds of smart pages in top 10 positions driving targeted traffic to all his websites, generating thousands of dollars every month.

HOW DIFFICULT ARE THEY TO CREATE?

Anyone who has created or *tried* to create smart pages knows how difficult and time consuming it is to edit the template provided (with Stephen's book) just to create a single smart page, not to mention that making one little mistake in one page can blow the whole deal.

It takes 10–20 minutes to create a single page if you are an experienced webmaster. You must multiply that by the *minimum* recommended 5–10 pages, not to mention the optimum recommended hundreds and even thousands of pages.

THIS TOOL CLAIMS TO HAVE ALL THE ANSWERS

There is a piece of software – *Targeted Traffic Machine* – that claims to do it all automatically. You can download it on a free trial basis and watch it spew out thousands of additional quality keywords and smart pages in seconds.

The benefits of using this software

1. Saves time.

2. Increases ranking and traffic.

3. You don't have to understand HTML to operate it.

4. Saves you from lethal errors that might prevent your website from getting the desired targeted traffic.

5. Maximises targeted traffic by automatically providing quality keywords.

6. Displays keyword search popularity automatically.

7. Generates unlimited smart pages, in a single click, within seconds.

8. Saves the keyword list to an ASCII file for future use.

9. Loads the keyword list from an ASCII file saved earlier, or a keyword list that was generated by another application.

10. Creates a site map with links to all the smart pages generated.

ARE SMART PAGES AS CLEVER AS THEY'RE CRACKED UP TO BE?

I don't know for sure but I'm beginning to believe they might be.

Having been a sceptic since I first heard about the concept I decided to put it to the test recently, but not wishing to invest in something that might not work, I downloaded the *Targeted Traffic Machine* smart pages creator on a 90-day free trial basis. The system itself is excellent but the Help section proves lamentably short on basic instruction. Undaunted I ploughed ahead and generated 70 pages of which 33 survived – because I didn't really know what I was doing I blew 50 per cent of my core pages and had to rebuild them not once but twice.

The good news is that all 33 surviving smart pages have now been listed by the major search engines and many of them have captured top ten slots. Daily traffic to my website has doubled but I don't credit the 'clever' pages entirely because I get lots of visitors from submitting articles.

The moral to my experiment

Try out smart pages generation for yourself but not until you are up to speed on what they are all about. Read Stephen Pierce's book where you will learn how, when, and why to use them. I didn't and caused myself needless anguish. Stephen should know – he invented the concept.

ALTERNATIVE SOFTWARE FOR GENERATING SMART PAGES

Here are the links for three alternative pieces of smart page generation software. I doubt they offer free trials and they will certainly prove more expensive to purchase. But you only get what you pay for.

www.smartpagegenerator.com

www.smartpagecreator.com

www.smartpagepro.com

20
How to avoid search engine positioning mistakes

When it comes to search engine optimisation there are certain common mistakes people make over and over again. Don't fall into this trap when preparing your own profitable retirement pursuit website (mini or maxi) for search engine submission. Here's a list of the 10 most common mistakes. By avoiding them you will also be avoiding a lot of anguish and frustration in the long run.

OPTIMISING YOUR SITE FOR THE WRONG KEYWORDS

The first step in any search engine optimisation campaign is to choose the keywords. We have already covered how to research and locate these, but we'll deal now with other vital considerations in relation to search engine implementation. If you initially choose the wrong keywords, all the time and effort that you devote in trying to get your site a high ranking will go down the drain. If you choose keywords which no one searches for, or if you choose keywords which won't bring in targeted traffic to your site, what good will the top rankings do for your retirement venture?

PUTTING TOO MANY KEYWORDS IN THE META TAG

I often see sites which have hundreds of keywords listed in the Meta Keywords tag in the hope that by listing the keywords in the Meta Keywords tag they will be able to get a high ranking for those keywords. Nothing could be further from the truth. Contrary to popular opinion, the Meta Keywords tag has almost completely lost its importance as far as search engine positioning is concerned. Hence, just by listing keywords in the Meta Keywords tag, you will never be able to get a high ranking. To get a high ranking for those keywords, you need to position them in the actual body content of your site, following the format detailed in Chapter 17.

REPEATING THE SAME KEYWORD TOO MANY TIMES

Another common mistake is endlessly to repeat target keywords in the body of pages and in the Meta Keywords tags. Because so many people have used this tactic in the past (and continue to use it), the search engines keep a sharp lookout, and may penalise a site which repeats keywords in this fashion. Sure, you do need to repeat the keywords a number of times. But, the way you place them in your pages must make grammatical sense. Simply repeating keywords endlessly is an exercise that no longer works. Furthermore, a particular keyword should ideally not be present more than three times in your Meta Keywords tag and your text.

USING HIDDEN TEXT

Hidden text is text with the same colour as the background colour of your page. For example, if the background colour of your page is white and you have added some white text to that page that is considered as hidden text.

This is how it works – or rather does *not* work – in practice.

Many webmasters in order to get high rankings in the search engines, try to make their pages as keyword rich as possible. However, there is a limit to the number of keywords you can repeat in a page without making it sound odd to your human visitors as they read the copy. Thus, in order to guarantee that visitors to a page don't perceive the text to be peculiar (but at the same time maintaining keyword rich content), some webmasters add text containing keywords in the same colour as the background colour. This ensures that while the search engines can see the keywords, the human visitors cannot. The search engines have long since caught up with this technique, and ignore or penalise the pages which contain such text. They may also penalise the *entire site* if even one of the pages in that site contains such hidden text. Don't use the hidden text technique; it's not worth it.

CREATING PAGES CONTAINING ONLY GRAPHICS

The search engines only understand text – they don't understand graphics. Hence, if your site contains lots of graphics but little text, it is unlikely to get a high ranking in the search engines. To improve your rankings, you need to replace the graphics by keyword-rich text for the search engine spiders to feed on.

ADDING KEYWORD-RICH TEXT TO THE 'NOFRAMES' TAG

Many search engines don't understand 'frames'. For sites which have used frames, these search engines only consider what is present in the NOFRAMES tag. Yet, many webmasters make the mistake of adding something like this to the NOFRAMES tag: 'This site uses frames but your browser doesn't support them'. For the search engines which don't understand frames, this is all the text that they ever get to see in this site, which means that the chances of this site getting a good ranking in these search engines are non-existent. Hence, if your site uses frames, you need to add a lot of keyword-rich text to the NOFRAMES tag.

USING PAGE CLOAKING

Page cloaking is a technique used to deliver different web pages under different circumstances. People generally use page cloaking for two reasons:

1. To hide the source code of their search engine optimised pages from their competitors.

2. To prevent human visitors from having to see a page which looks good to the search engines but does not necessarily look good to them.

The problem with this is that when a site uses the cloaking technique it prevents the search engines from being able to spider the same page that their users are going to see. And if the search engines can't do this they can no longer be confident of providing relevant results to their users. Thus, if a search engine discovers that a site has used cloaking it will probably ban the site forever from their index. Hence, my advice is that you should not even think about using cloaking in your site.

USING AUTOMATIC SUBMISSION TOOLS

In order to save time many people use a run-of-the-mill automatic submission software or service to submit their sites to the major search engines. It is true that submitting your site manually to the search engines takes a lot of time and that an automatic submission tool can help you save a lot of time. However, the search engines don't like these tools and may ignore your pages if you use them. In my opinion the major search engines are simply too important for you not to spend the time to submit your site manually – that is if you decide not to do what I'm suggesting next.

There is a legitimate way to avoid this tiresome process. When you host your website with either *Third Sphere* or *Site Build It!* they do it all for you at no extra cost. What's more, the automatic software they use is state of the art and perfectly acceptable to the major search engines.

SUBMITTING TOO MANY PAGES DAILY

People often make the mistake of submitting too many pages per day to the search engines. This often results in the search engines simply ignoring many of the pages which have been submitted from that site. Ideally, you should submit no more than one page per day to the search engines. While many search engines accept more than one page per day from a particular domain there are some majors which do not. Hence, by limiting yourself to a maximum of one page per day you ensure that you stay within the limits of all the search engines.

DEVOTING TOO MUCH TIME TO SEARCH ENGINE POSITIONING

Here's the final common mistake that people make when it comes to search engine optimisation – they spend too much time over it when they opt to do it manually. Sure, search engine placement is the most cost effective way of driving traffic to your site and you do need to spend some time every day learning how the search engines work in optimising your site. However, you must remember that search engine optimisation is a means to an end for you – it's not the end in itself. The end is to increase the sales of your products and services. Hence, apart from trying to improve your site's position in the search engines, you also need to spend time on all the other factors which determine the success or the failure of your website: the quality of the products and services that you are selling, the quality of your customer service, and so on. You may have excellent rankings in the search engines but if the quality of your produce is poor, or if your customer service leaves a lot to be desired, those high rankings aren't going to do much good.

CLOSING THOUGHT

I appreciate that all of the foregoing will come across as a great deal to take on board when you're retired and trying to add to your basic income. But look at it this way: even if you decide to do it all automatically using one of my preferred hosting options you still need to understand the basics if you are to appreciate the results. I do. Why not you?

21
Flooding your site with low- and no-cost traffic

The bulk of the traffic to your website will come from the major search engines but there are several other low and no-cost avenues to explore and if used correctly and regularly they can flood your site with traffic.

PAY-PER-CLICK (PPC) SEARCH ENGINES

Search engine optimisation is a skilled exercise with no guarantee of sustained success for even the most competitive keywords. Equally, paid submissions cannot guarantee top positions for your web pages; they can only guarantee indexing in the search engine database. You may still come up in the hundredth page of search results.

These factors have made pay-per-click search engines an important element of any website promotion campaign. Actually, these engines could also be called pay-for-position search engines. You could bid for the number one position in search results for the keyword you choose. If there are many bidders you would have to bid high (in pounds instead of pence for every single visitor to secure a top position). You then pay at the bid rate for every click-through to your website (hence … 'pay-per-click').

The best strategy for the PPC element of your campaign is to bid for a number of less competitive keywords that are important to you. This could be significantly less expensive than bidding for one high-competition keyword. Finding bid prices for the keywords, submitting bids for all these, and then tracking the results for each is a tedious exercise. However, there are tools to automate much of this tiresome work and with one of these, you could focus on selecting the keywords to bid for and leave the rest to the tool.

NEWSGROUP, FORUM, AND MAILING LIST PARTICIPATION

The second tactic is to participate in targeted forums and newsgroups on their specific topic. It's free. You start visiting the forum regularly and then once you know your way around it you should start answering questions for people and becoming an all-round helpful individual. Give and it will be given back to you.

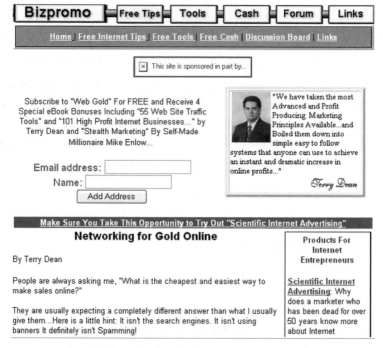

Fig. 11. Participating in forums to attract traffic.

You will be able to build up relationships in these forums and build up your traffic at the same time without ever having to spend a penny. To find out more about how to participate in forums for maximum traffic, check out this free report:

www.netofficetoolbox.com

The best places to find the actual forums and newsgroups are:

- **Forums** can be found at www.forumone.com.
- **Newsgroups** can be searched at www.groups.google.com.
- **Mailing lists** are found at www.liszt.com.

TRADING LINKS WITH OTHER WEBSITES

Another no-cost marketing technique is to trade links with other websites. Now, I know from experience this can be a daunting task at first – you trade 10 links and only get a small volume of traffic from it – but what happens when you start having hundreds or thousands of *related sites* linked to you? You get a flood of visitors, that's what.

Where do you start? Start by getting out there and offering; offer to trade links with people who are in the same forums, newsgroups, and mailing lists as you. Go to some of the online databases that have links. Participate in banner exchanges and link exchanges. Nothing will happen unless you take the initiative and do something.

For top resources in this area, check out:

www.whitepalm.com/fourcorners/linkswapping.shtml

www.netofficetoolbox.com

We'll be covering the power of linking in greater detail in Chapter 25.

WRITING ARTICLES FOR EZINES AND MAGAZINES

There are thousands of ezines and magazines out there just waiting for your articles. Whatever your area of expertise, write about it or if you don't want to do the writing yourself, collect the information together in an organised manner and have someone else do it for you. Once you have your highly informative article ready to go, contact publishers of ezines and magazines and submit your piece. Think about the publicity you can get through this. It can bring thousands of people to your site with almost no cost at all.

For information on ezines, check out:

www.refer-me.com/members/e-zine-master/.

For the top media directory for offline publications see:

www.gebbieinc.com.

In Chapter 24 I'll let you in on my own secrets on how to milk this no-cost method to attract thousands of targeted visitors to your retirement opportunity website.

USING CGI TRAFFIC PLUG-INS ON YOUR SITE

There are many CGI programmes out there which can become traffic generators by having your visitors return over and over again. Tools such as classified ad sites, free-for-all link pages, message boards, chat rooms, postcard sites, and more can all contribute to your overall traffic building plan. Many of these programmes can be added to your website for little or no money. Take a look at this resource for finding these types of scripts:

www.cgi-resources.com/Programs_and_Scripts/Perl.

For many people though, installing a CGI programme may be a nightmare. For those of you who are technically challenged, CGI Resource has a list of places where you can have your traffic plug-ins remotely hosted for you. Check out their remotely hosted scripts at: www.cgi-resources.com.

THE POWER OF FREE PRESS RELEASES

Don't just think it takes knowing the right people to get your press releases out. It doesn't. If you can give the media stories which are interesting and revealing, they will be glad to publish them.

- Do you have a new exciting product?

- Do you have an event going on at your site that's newsworthy?

Come up with one and then contact the media.

Here are two services I use where you can do it all for free:

www.prweb.com

www.free-press-release.com

When someone asks you to pay out money for an ad (as they will), check back on these ways to advertise your site for little or no cost. Many of them can create awesome traffic at your site and don't cost a penny. The ones which do have a small cost to them can produce traffic worth far more than many of the ads out there.

To promote an internet website does not require a large advertising budget. Those who have a large budget at their disposal also labour under a big disadvantage when marketing online; they pay for ad after ad and end up losing most of their money. Online, the best things in life are free.

22
Why you must test-market every task you undertake

Any good marketer knows that testing is the key to building profits in absolutely any business. You can never determine that one idea will or will not work in any specific business until you put it to the test. Don't think that the internet is any different.

- You have to test products.
- You have to test prices.
- You have to test promotional formats.
- You have to test headlines.
- You have to test ad copy.
- You have to test specific places to promote.

The testing process never ends. If you don't put your entire marketing plan to the test you will never truly know what can or cannot work in your niche retirement pursuit. Every marketing test is an investment in your venture whether it produces results for you or not. It shows either a marketing method to keep working with or a method to avoid in your specific type of business. Take every single test you use as another lesson in your marketing education.

ARE YOU INVESTING OR GAMBLING IN YOUR NICHE RETIREMENT OPPORTUNITY?

The core problem in marketing presents itself when you start treating your advertising more like a gamble than an investment. Most internet businesses are just haphazardly wasting their money on every advertising opportunity that comes up. They don't key their ads and they don't take notes about what is working and why it is working. For some reason or other, the majority of marketers have developed an idea that the internet is somehow different from other promotional mediums. They think that if they just try enough different techniques, they may just magically come upon the technique that will make lots of money.

You can't just throw your money into promotion. You need to have a plan behind everything you do. You need to know when a technique is working so that you can run with it. You need to know what isn't working. Setting up the right testing mechanisms is the key to success in your marketing. You can't afford to gamble away whatever you earn from promotion.

How much does your website make per visitor?

If you don't know the answer to this question then it isn't even possible for you to make informed decisions about what types of promotion you can use.

DETERMINING HOW MUCH TO SPEND ON WEBSITE VISITORS

If you don't know how much your website makes per visitor on average, how can you determine how much to spend to obtain each visitor? If your website brings in an average of a £1.00 per visitor, then you can afford to spend a lot more per visitor than a site which is bringing in only five pence per visitor. When you are using free advertising for your site you may not consider this to be very important, but once you start spending some of your cash flow on marketing, I can guarantee that if you don't know how much your site makes per visitor you are just working on a gamble.

ADDING UP YOUR INCOME AND UNIQUE VISITORS

The simplest method of determining your profit per visitor is to just add up your website income and all of your unique hits from the past month. Then divide the income by the number of visits you have received. That will give you a baseline number to get started with. As you start testing promotion more and more, you are also going to want to determine how many hits and how much profit you get from each type of ad. All visits are not created equal. Offline advertising will produce fewer visits than many types of online marketing, but usually they are of a much better quality than promotional formats such as banner ads. These offline visitors end up buying more stuff and having a much higher profit per visitor.

Your site could be making £2.00 per visitor from offline advertising and only 20p per visitor from banner ads. Getting those two types of visitors mixed up could cause you to make some very bad decisions about your advertising. That is where keying your ads and testing comes in. You must convert your promotion into a scientific investment instead of a haphazard gamble. You can do this most effectively by following a simple three-step system like the one I will show you below. It is the key to knowing which mediums are working for you – and which ones aren't.

SETTING UP A WEBSITE TRACKING SYSTEM

The first thing you will have to do to start finding out what type of advertising works for you is to set up some kind of tracking system. If you aren't tracking your visitors, then you can just forget about making intelligent marketing decisions. Also note that you need to be tracking more than just the overall traffic of your site. You need to know where people are going to on your site and you need each of your web pages tracked as well.

There are three simple ways to track your website stats:

1. You can use a free counter for each page on your website.

2. You can install a CGI program to track your stats.

3. You can purchase your domain where stats are part of the package.

USING A FREE COUNTER FOR EACH PAGE

Superstats is the counter I use and recommend to you. The advantage of this method is that it is pretty simple to set up. You sign up for their service and then you insert their code into your site.

The disadvantage is that you will have a small link back to them on your site which may cost you a little traffic. An even bigger disadvantage is that you will need to sign up and insert a separate code on every one of your pages so that each page can be tracked separately. Having overall domain stats won't do you that much good if you don't know where they are coming from and who the buyers are.

v2.superstats.com/

INSTALLING A CGI PROGRAM TO TRACK YOUR STATS

There are over 70 CGI programmes out there which will track your stats for you. Make sure that you choose a program that tracks your stats on each page of your site. You don't want to have to use a separate CGI program for each page and you don't want all of your pages put together.

The advantage of using a CGI program is that you won't have to lose any traffic to outside sources and that some of the CGI programmes can track all of your pages separately for you in one file. The disadvantage of this method is that it requires some programming knowledge and is often quite difficult to set up.

For a list of website counter programs, visit cgi.resourceindex.com/.

PURCHASING DOMAINS WHERE STATS ARE PART OF THE DEAL

On my own current web hosts, stats for every single page of my sites are included. We talked about these particular hosting services in Chapter 16 but to refresh your memory, they are *Third Sphere* and *Site Build It!*

• Top pages are listed.

• Error messages that people receive are listed.

• Unique hits and page impressions for every single page are listed separately in these easy-to-use systems.

The essential advantage is that these are advanced tracking systems and simple to operate.

KEYING ALL YOUR PROMOTIONAL EFFORTS

You need to key all of your ads separately. The easiest way to do this is to make a copy of your sales letter on your site and create another site out of it. If your sales letter is named sales.htm, you could also make a sales1.htm, sales2.htm, sales3.htm, and so on. Then, use a different page as your website address for each ad you put out (much like the smart page technique we discussed in Chapter 19).

If you really want to track your advertising results effectively, you will also want to make copies of your order form. Then, you can know which ad is actually producing the sales and exactly how much money is coming in from every penny you spend. There are some other methods you could use to key your ads. For example, you could also set up an affiliate programme on your site and allocate each one a different affiliate number for each ad you place. This would automatically track all the sales for you. You could use different auto-responders for the responses. If you are doing a major offline advertising campaign, you could even set up a complete duplicate domain that you don't advertise any other way.

No matter which method you choose to use, the important thing is that you key and track every single one of your ads.

JUDGING YOUR RESULTS AND EXPANDING YOUR PROMOTION

After you have placed each ad, judge how it does. Did it produce a profit for you? If not, do you know why it didn't work? Try changing the headline, the body copy, or the advertising medium. Make only one of these changes at a time. If you change everything at once you will never know which aspect it was that created the change in results. If your ad did produce a profit, how can you expand on it? Try changing the headline or the ad slightly and see what the results are. Find other similar places that you could use to expand your advertising. Do this in a slow methodical way so you can track and keep increasing your profits with every ad you place.

If every ad you place is losing money then you are going to need to step back and re-examine your product, your market, your USP, and your overall concepts.

Are you selling what your market really wants and is it better than the competition?

Advertising never has to be a gamble. It can be an intelligent investment that will produce results for you time and time again. Look at the mutual fund manager. They may have 20 or more different stocks in their portfolio. While some of the stocks may lose money, the idea is to keep most of them making a profit.

- By combining all of the different stocks in one portfolio, they can reduce the risks and increase their chances of profit.

- By tracking all of your ads and using different forms of advertising, you can reduce your overall risk and then expand on whichever advertising pulls in the most profits.

Don't ever look at your retirement pursuit as a get rich quick scheme or you will end up gambling away your advertising budget. Look at yourself as the mutual fund manager who intelligently picks and chooses the right sources for his or her portfolio.

Invest wisely in your profitable retirement pursuit.

If you're thinking this is an almighty amount of work to be undertaking in retirement, it is. But if you do it, and do it consistently, you will make money online. You will also increase your awareness and add years to your lifespan.

23
How to use digitised books to sell your expertise

Now you are about to discover just how easy it is to convert your expertise into the first digitised produce for your profitable retirement pursuit, how to package it, how to market it, but before we start check that you have:

- got it all down on paper;

- explained the methodology;

- listed the features;

- highlighted the benefits;

- established what you don't know about your topic;

- rectified the information shortfall by researching;

- researched until you've located all you still needed to learn;

- identified your market;

- discovered how to reach it;

- learned how to test market;

- committed to learning how to promote.

If you are in any doubt about any item on this list go back to Chapter 2 for refreshment and then come back here.

CREATING YOUR OWN DIGITAL INFORMATION PRODUCE

It's as easy as pie. Once you are completely satisfied with the text for your project you simply pop it into the software compiler of your choice and out comes the finished information product. You can include graphics, illustrations, pictures, flow charts, etc. – whatever you reckon will add glitz to the overall effect.

Choice of systems

For formatting you have a choice of …

- EXE (short for *Executable Extension* and pronounced ee-ex-ee) – is an executable file with an .exe extension.

- PDF (short for *Portable Document Format*) – a file format developed by Adobe Systems. PDF captures formatting information from a variety of desktop publishing applications, making it possible to send formatted documents and have them appear on the recipient's monitor or printer as they were intended. To view a file in PDF format, you need Adobe Reader, a free application distributed by Adobe Systems (www.adobe.com).

EXE produces complete documents in minutes whereas PDF does the same job in *seconds*. Of the two, my personal preference is PDF and not just because it's faster; it also provides a more polished finish, it can be read on any computer screen anywhere in the world – and it's cheaper; sometimes completely free.

Compiler for EXE production

www.ebookgenerator.com

This is quite expensive to purchase.

Compiler options for PDF production

Be careful shopping around for PDF compilers. You can get ripped off mercilessly by fly-by-night shysters telling how difficult the system is to master and trying to sell you expensive instruction courses. It's not at all difficult; it is simplicity itself.

Here are the compilers I use for my information produce. They are excellent and for both you are allowed to create your first e-books for free.

- *Adobe PDF Online* – free trial/5 e-books/100MB capacity for each book. Access it at www.adobe.com.

- *docudesk* – same deal but thereafter $19.95 (approx. £11) for permanent usage. www.docudesk.com.

Explore the alternative systems for compilation and decide for yourself with which you feel the most comfortable.

Have this one on me ...

I recently purchased an excellent e-book on the subject of digitising information produce. *Simple Guide to Creating e-books* is the title and it cost me $49.95 – but you, dear valued reader, can have it for *free*. Here is what to do: visit my website www.writing-for-profit.com. Click on the button marked 'FREE eBOOK' in the navigation bar, fill in a simple form, and the download link for your free copy (plus 2 bonus books) will be emailed straight back to you.

CREATING VIRTUAL BOOK COVERS AUTOMATICALLY

When your first e-book rolls off the assembly line you will want to wrap it in a professionally produced cover and, until recently, design and creation would have set you back between £75 and £125 per cover. Not any more. There are now several software tools available that do it all for you.

How important is it to have a cover for your information product?

Very important, and here's why. When people browse around bookstores the first thing to capture their attention is the cover. That's stage one in the decision-making process: to buy or not to buy. The same thing applies with online browsers on the lookout for virtual books to purchase, and you will greatly enhance your chances of success if all your e-produce is appropriately packaged. After all, who buys a book, offline or online, without an opportunity of glancing at the cover to discover what's inside?

Here are two examples of the best in e-book cover generation software.

• *eBook Cover Generator* – Costs $97 (approx. £54) to purchase outright. No free trial. www.ebookcovergenerator.com

• *Virtual Cover Creator* – Costs $67 (approx. £37) but offers an unlimited free trial to enable you to become familiar with the package. You won't be able to use the end produce in the trial version because it will be watermarked until you pay for it. www.virtualcovercreator.com

My personal preference is for the latter option which I use for all my e-produce.

DEVISING THE STRATEGY FOR SALES AND DISTRIBUTION

We covered the bones of this in Chapter 6 but you will be provided in Chapter 30 with a detailed strategy for automatic order-taking and product fulfilment. Suffice to say here that when you have everything else in position, sales and distribution form the simplest aspect of the exercise.

WHY IT PAYS TO GIVE E-BOOKS AWAY FOR FREE

Believe it or not you will sell more information products online if you start by giving some away for free. Here is how it works. You have created your first e-book, set the price, automated order-taking and distribution, and are raring to go. What you do now is to produce a mini 'taster' version to give away free of charge to your website visitors. You should start the taster with a 'flat' book cover (don't worry, the software shows you how to do this), followed by your preface or introduction, one or two sample chapters, and culminating in your entire sales page complete with ordering instructions. Most people will pick up anything for free online and you will be amazed how many are persuaded to purchase directly from the taster. You are dealing with targeted prospects and giving them two bites at the cherry. It's like allowing them to turn the pages as they would in a physical bookstore.

Have a look at how I do it when you call at writing-for-profit.com to collect the free information produce I promised you. Better still, proceed then to visit my main website howtoproducts-xl.com where you can view a panorama of e-covers for my personally generated produce.

WHEN YOU CHOOSE TO SELL SOMEONE ELSE'S PRODUCE

Okay, so you still don't want to roll out your own produce. Does that mean you are excluded? No! You have many options if you decide you want to sell someone else's information produce – and here are two of the best.

The first concerns affiliate reselling and if you visit this site www.associateprograms.com you will discover hundreds of opportunities.

The second is a ready-made turnkey publishing business where you can enjoy all of the following benefits for a monthly membership fee of $27 (approx. £15).

1. *The Resale Rights Cooperative*™ – Acquire the marketing rights to $1,000s worth of brand new digital information and software products on demand, and without purchasing them.

2. *Instant Turnkey Business Packages* – Gain instant access to a wide variety of 100 per cent profit online products and turnkey business packages.

3. *Ebook of the Month Club*™ – Every month you receive a new e-book or software product with members-only branding features, and full marketing rights.

4. *The Internet Marketing Database*™ – Use the world's only copyright-free database of internet marketing related information to create your very own digital information products in as little as 60 minutes each.

5. *The Wholesale Product Locator*™ – Locate and acquire just about any type of product you'd like to sell online at the lowest price available.

6. *Premium Web Hosting* – Ad free, fast and reliable web hosting featuring 500 Megs of space and 10 Gigs of transfer.

7. *Unlimited Pro Auto-responders – Unlimited Push-Button Responders*™ (sequential auto-responder accounts), each featuring unlimited automated messaging, list broadcasting, personalised messages, etc.

8. *Instant Ad Tracker*™ – Determine which of your ads are successful, and weed out those that are not. Track up to 1,000 different links.

9. *The Internet Marketing Cooperative*™ – Request and receive new internet marketing related products without paying a penny extra. Grow your knowledge and your online business.

10. *The PBP Marketing Forum*™ – A flourishing community of online business owners anxious to field questions and share ideas.

Plus these free bonuses when you become a member:

- Instant access to the *PBP™* Master Tutorial – shows you, step by step, how to use *PBP™* services and resources to build your own web empire. You'll learn how to build a responsive list of subscribers. You'll discover how to build an unlimited residual income with affiliate and MLM programmes. You'll learn how to create your own profitable website.

- 24/7 access to the easy to use *ULTRA Web Page Creator™* (HTML editor) – Create unlimited web pages from any location with a computer and internet access; $12.95 monthly value, free to members.

- Affiliate tracking script. Unlimited auto-responder script – traffic exchange script. Safelist script and *much* more. You could create endless complete web businesses with these scripts, and, for example, sell the businesses on eBay™ for huge profits. The possibilities are truly endless.

- Personal consulting through members' forum – value unlimited, but free to members.

  www.pushbuttonpublishing.com

HOW TO CREATE YOUR OWN SOFTWARE PROGRAMS

Even if you don't know how to write a single line of code you can create your own exclusive software programs in 30 minutes or your money back, according to the vendors. This startling new invention (patent pending) creates an infinite number of high-demand software programs which you can sell royalty-free at any price.

You can access complete details of this amazing new tool by visiting this website: www.MakeYourOwnSoftware.com/bestsellers.

24
Exploiting the amazing
power of articles

All successful e-entrepreneurs use articles to lure visitors to their websites. They cost nothing but time and energy to produce and distribute, and the power they exert is astounding. *Article submission is the perfect niche vehicle for attracting pre-qualified, targeted prospects for your niche produce.*

- You should adopt this influential practice for your retirement pursuit;

- You will miss out on a goldmine of potential buyers if you do not.

You know all there is to know about your first project; you even produced an information product on the topic. Now is the time to make a start on your first batch of articles.

WHERE TO START?

Do as you did to create your taster e-book. Pull down strands of useful information from every chapter of your information product; sculpt it into a dozen or so initial articles for distribution (I'll show you how, why and where in a moment). When you think you've exhausted that source, go back to your research notes and you will find more, much more. When you've finished doing that, go back online and research again. Look at what other people have to say about the topic; not to copy them, but to use whatever you glean to prompt you to search in different directions. Then do likewise at discussion forums. The supply of information is endless.

WRITING YOUR FIRST ARTICLE FOR DISTRIBUTION

You will get the hang of it very quickly and when you do, you will be churning out one or two articles at a time, quite effortlessly. There are just a few simple rules to observe:

1. Start with an eye-grabbing headline.

2. Fire your biggest gun in the first sentence.

3. Fire the next biggest in the next sentence or two.

4. Keep the text rolling on with short chunky paragraphs.

5. Break it up with occasional sub-headings.

6. Keep it conversational.

7. Restrict the word count to between 500 and 700.

8. End with a resource box (your bio).

Here now is a text example of one of my own articles which is shown again in published format in Figure 12.

Fact: Start a Business Without A Masterplan For Success And You Are 95 Per Cent Certain to Fail!

Fact: *Only five per cent of People Who Start a Business Make it into Year Six.*

'95 per cent of small business start-ups fail within five years. Two-thirds of new employer firms survive at least two years, and about half survive at least four years.' (Source: Small Business Administration 2004.)

How can this be when the same US Government source claims that small firms represent more than 99.7 per cent of all employers? Why is the failure rate so high? Here's why: 95 per cent of all start-ups have no masterplan in place at the outset and in consequence flounder and sink without a trace. What's more, this alarming fatality level applies to offline and online enterprises equally. Even worse, tens of thousands more start a business every day and follow exactly the same route to disaster.

Fact: Google lists in excess of 12,000,000 websites offering advice on how to start a business – but how many I wonder emanate from people who've actually done it for themselves. My site does. I've founded, owned and operated dozens of small businesses – and I'm still doing it. I've also authored two widely-acclaimed bestselling hard copy books on the topic, *Starting Your Own Business* (How To Books ISBN 1-85703-859-2) and *Starting an Internet Business at Home* (Kogan Page ISBN 0-7494-3484-8); titles that sell in big numbers online at Amazon.com and offline in bookstores throughout the world.

Now I'm unzipping my case notes spanning forty years of successful independent commercial activity to present you with an all-in-one masterplan to ensure success before you start a business – and to maintain momentum in tandem with your endeavors so that you don't end up in the same place as 95 per cent of start-ups: the dump truck.

The All-in-One Start a Business Masterplan doesn't simply focus on getting you up and running. As the Ultimate Start a Business Compendium it goes deeper, much deeper. In its four individual tutorials it aims at the creative heart of operating a small enterprise: how to start a business with failsafe offline and online strategies, how to avoid the crucial mistakes that cripple 95 per cent of all start-ups, and how to sustain progress with tried, tested, proven stratagems.

Blueprint for fulfilment before you start a business

The All-in-One Start a Business Masterplan will empower you to conceive your own exclusive blueprint for a happy, successful and rewarding small business operation. Plans are great things. They show you where you are going, what to do, and how to do it when you get there. Make no mistake though; you will not be creating this blueprint just to get you started. It's going to be around for a long time and you will want to review and update it regularly to take account of twists and turns along the way. That's the beauty of it. When you have a blueprint for success, you can legislate for change. Without one you cannot; you'll be like the explorer in the jungle without a map.

The all-in-one start a business masterplan

What this is not is a hotchpotch of miscellaneous lame-brained notions and opinions cobbled together to create a sycophantic litany. The All-in-One Start a Business Masterplan is the genuine product of my own personal experience as a successful small business owner offline and online. It consists of four comprehensive tutorials, 60 full blown chapters, 555 pages, and covers every aspect of single-minded entrepreneurship: galvanizing into initial action, getting started on your plan, settling on an idea for your enterprise, tackling initial teething problems, overcoming the threatening scenarios everyone encounters along the way, and setting the course for a lifetime of fulfilment and enrichment. The good, the bad, and the in-between are all recorded: where I hit the target plumb centre, where I screwed up, and how I put it right.

Jim Green is a successful networker and bestselling author with a string of niche non-fiction titles to his credit. His All-In-One Tutorial is available at www.writing-for-profit.com/start-a-business.html.

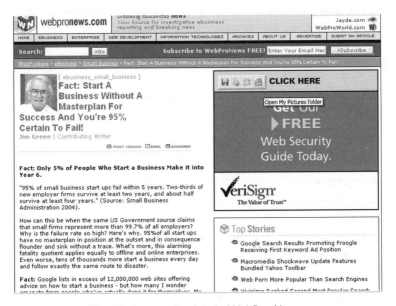

Fig. 12. Featured article in WebPro News.

This article appeared in *Web Pro News* (the leading online magazine) and attracted 2071 additional visitors to my website in just 14 days.

WORST-CASE SCENARIO FOR PUBLISHED ARTICLES

Does promoting with articles always work to drive huge numbers of visitors to your site instantly every single time you do it? No. The truth is not every single article you write and distribute online will hit a home run and bring an avalanche of visitors to your site. Some of my articles only attract a trickle but I have so many of them out there now that in total they add up to a sizeable volume of steady, targeted traffic. Periodically I hit a grand slam with an article that takes on a life of its own and dumps thousands of visitors on my site in a couple of days – like the one you just read.

Here's the worst thing that can happen with every article you publish:

- You continue to **build** your reputation and credibility with your target audience as a trusted expert.

- As your **credibility** increases, joint venture partners will begin to seek you out and be open to your approaches.

- You'll create additional tools your affiliates can use to **sell more** of your products.

- You create more **valuable content** for your own and other people's websites that the search engines can index – **driving even more traffic** to your website or affiliate link.

- You create additional instalments for your auto-responder series that you can easily turn into **profitable** mini-courses.

- You get better and better at picking topics, distributing articles and your traffic logs will **snowball with targeted visitors**.

In fact, just by writing and distributing free articles on the internet (something that becomes pretty easy once you start), you will become recognised as a world-class expert on the topic of your choice and you will have people seeking you out for all kinds of lucrative opportunities.

- Promoting with articles represents one of the best ways to not only attract free traffic but to build your business and your reputation online.

WHERE TO SUBMIT YOUR ARTICLE OUTPUT FOR FREE

And now to save you the time and trouble of doing it yourself, I will give you my own list of 'hubs' for article submission. You can add to this as you discover other outlets relevant to your specialist topic.

Article hubs that accept your material and distribute it for free

ezinearticles.com
www.certificate.net/wwio
www.ideamarketers.com
www.marketing-seek.com
www.goarticles.com
www.netterweb.com
www.articlesfactory.com
www.worldabooks.com/writers-connection/
www.web-source.net/syndicator_submit.htm
www.searchwarp.com
www.etext.org
www.zinos.com
www.addme.com
www.vectorcentral.com
www.webpronews.com
www.writersdigest.com
www.linksnoop.com
www.articlehub.com
www.freelancewriting.com/newssyndicator.html
writingcorner.com/admin/sub-guidelines.htm
www.abundancecenter.com

theezine.net
www.home-based-business-opportunities.com/library/id2101-book.shtml
www.entrepreneurnewz.com
www.homebasedbusinessindex.com
www.homeincome.com

THIS SOFTWARE DOES IT ALL AUTOMATICALLY

It's called *Ezine Announcer* but it works equally well for distributing articles in bulk to all recognised sources. A new enhanced model was recently introduced and last time I looked it cost $67 (approx. £37) to purchase. It is also available on an extended free trial basis.

www.articleannouncer.com/

USING PRESS RELEASES FOR DISTRIBUTION

We talked about press releases in an earlier chapter where I provided you with two excellent sources for distribution. While you will come across lots of advice elsewhere regarding formatting I recommend you stick with what I've just given you on construction. It works for me and it will work for you.

25
The power of linking to other websites

Another clever cost-free way of driving traffic to your retirement opportunity website is through the power of linking to other sites; not any old sites, but sites specifically related to your topic. Take the trouble to sniff them out by undertaking some basic research. Try this out for size at the Google search engine: 'your topic + websites' and again 'your topic + articles' (replacing of course 'your topic' with your own particular topic). You will be presented with a myriad of potential linking partners but you won't be linking to all of them because that would defeat the purpose: link only to those (100/125 maximum) that you sense relate most closely to your website content. Link to too many and the search engines won't be happy.

I have 114 quality links to my prime site and they consistently bring in targeted traffic that I wouldn't otherwise get.

TEN EASY STEPS FOR BUILDING YOUR LINK POPULARITY

You did your homework and learned all about optimising techniques for your website. Your relevant keywords are prominently placed in all the right places on your pages. Yet your site still isn't ranking the way you want.

- What do you do?
- Why bother with link building?

Link popularity and link quality are very important because every major search engine now considers them as a part of their ranking algorithms. If you don't have links you won't rank well for competitive keywords. If your page includes all the important on-the-page criteria and scores well with Alexa it's time to focus on your links. Good inbound links can move your page up the ranking ladder and act as new entry points to your site. But how does your site get those coveted inbound links we hear so much about?

First off, let's make sure you understand the basics.

- Link popularity is the measure of inbound links to your website.

- Link analysis evaluates which sites are linking to you and the link text itself.

Fortunately, there are many ways to improve your link quality and popularity, which will give you a boost in the rankings. Here are some guidelines to help you set up your own linking campaign.

1 – Prepare your site first

Before you start your link-building campaign, take time to get your site in shape. Make sure your site looks professional, has good content and is easy to navigate. Check your links with a tool like www.htmltoolbox.com. If a potential linker goes to your site and finds broken pages, they are not going to want to link to you. In addition, directories have gone on record saying they may exclude sites with broken links and page errors. Directories want only professional looking sites in their databases so do your homework on your site before you start promoting it and your linking campaign will be more effective.

2 – Allow time for link building

Don't expect to grow your link popularity overnight. Allow time every week to work on link building. If you force yourself to spend a couple of hours a week on the project, it will become part of your routine.

Pick one day a week and set aside time as your link-building time. If you don't make it a priority, it won't get done. Link building is an incremental activity. Over time these one or two new links start adding up until they are into the hundreds.

3 – Establish realistic link goals

Don't expect to see instant results. Link building is difficult, frustrating and time intensive. Convincing another website to link to you can be exasperating. If you get one good quality link a month you're doing better than the majority of sites out there. Patience and creativity are germane to link building.

- Track your progress so you know who you've asked already. It could be embarrassing to ask a site for a link if they've already given you one.

- If a website initially declines your link request, wait a while and then ask again. Their focus may change over time. A 'no' today may change into a 'yes' six to nine months later.

4 – Link popularity is all about quality

Be selective about the sites from which you request links. Search engines use sophisticated rules when judging the importance of a link and the popularity of the site linking to you is a key criterion. One link from CNet.com or bbc.co.uk is worth much more than ten links from a personal website (I have a link to BBC Headlines at www.howtoproducts-xl.com and it brings me 25–30 additional visitors every day). And don't even think of using a 'link farm'. Link farms are sites that exist solely to link to other websites. They are nothing more than a blatant attempt to inflate link popularity, and search engines take a dim view of them. Google in particular has been known to ban sites found using a link farm.

Try to identify non-competitive sites in the same field as your site. Links from sites that are related to your area carry more weight than sites from Aunt Sue's fashion site. That doesn't mean you should refuse a link from Aunt Sue; just be aware it won't help you much in link quality terms. On the other hand, links from sites within the orbit of your own specialist topic are strong endorsements for your site.

5 – Develop a relationship with a site

Before you ask for the link, get to know the website. Establish yourself as a real human first. That way, when you ask for a link, it's harder for them to say no. Impersonal broadcast emails asking for links are spam. Sure, it's easier, but it will only result in making another website owner mad at you. Spam link requests do not work and waste everyone's time. Don't do it.

6 – Provide the linking code

Make it easy for other sites to link to you. Send the prospective linker the exact HTML code you want in the link and suggest which page you want the link from. This ensures the right words are used in the link and reduces the burden in setting up the link. Everybody on the internet is pressed for time and if you don't make it simple by giving them the exact HTML, you've made their job too hard. Make it easy and your success rate will go up.

7 – Get directory listings

Jumpstart your link campaign by getting directory links first; this is especially important if you have a new site or a site with no inbound links. A shortage of inbound links puts your site at a severe disadvantage because link analysis is an important part of every search engine's ranking algorithm. The way to overcome this is to get a few quality links. A good way to start is to get listed in as many directories as you can. There are many directories out there, and the more you can get into the better.

A few to target include:

1. Open Directory.

2. Yahoo!

3. LookSmart.

4. Zeal.com.

5. Joeant.com.

6. Business.com.

Be aware that most of these directories (except the first one listed) require you to pay for a listing but it's worth the expense if you can afford it.

8 – Consider bartering for links

It's a good idea to have something to offer in return for a link. Many sites won't link to you unless you link back to them or otherwise make it worth their while. Create a Resources or Partner page that allows you to have a place from which you can easily link to them. You might also offer to work a barter arrangement with them. If you have a site popular with their target market they might consider free advertisements in exchange for a link. If the link is of great value to you be prepared to give something back.

9 – Link building alternative

If time constraints keep you from link building consider outsourcing your link popularity work. Link building is undoubtedly the most time consuming part of search engine optimisation. You may find it is not cost effective to do it yourself. That doesn't mean you shouldn't do it, it just means you hire someone else to do it for you.

Cautionary note: if you do chose to hire a company specialising in link building make sure they follow good link-building practices. Ask them to describe the process they use to request links. Make certain they follow a personalised approach and don't simply spam sites with requests for links. If they refuse to discuss their link building methods you can assume they use impersonal widespread email drops or link farms – that's spam. They may give it a sophisticated name, but if the process involves sending out large numbers of form emails, it's still spam and will only set your campaign backwards and injure your reputation. Go and find a different company or better still, develop the links you need yourself. I've always done it; I've never spent a penny on the linking process.

10 – Just do it!

Link popularity is important and the link-building process needs to be given high priority. Link analysis is only going to get more important to search engines, not less. Search engines have found it highly resistant to manipulation and a legitimate way to measure the importance of a site. Since link building takes time, the sooner you start the better.

So think of link building as a long-term investment in your site. Put in a little time now to improve your linking today to insure a good search engine ranking in the future.

HOW RECIPROCAL LINKING INCREASES WEBSITE EFECTIVENESS

1. Other websites send you visitors because they link to you. If you have just 10 links pointing to your site and each site sends you on average only two visitors per day, you will only achieve 20 targeted prospects. **Work at building your linking partners so that you attract much higher levels of targeted traffic.**

2. Search engines like Google and Teoma use link popularity to rank websites. If your site has high link popularity then you will be rewarded with high rankings. **To improve your link popularity you must have reciprocal links.**

3. Exchanging reciprocal links with other sites in your niche will build a valuable links directory. **Visitors will bookmark your**

website and visit you frequently because you can offer them a valuable resource: your links directory. The most frequented of my own pages is 'Resources' (see below) where my directory is located. My visitors love it and keep coming back for more.

COMBINING ARTICLES AND LINKS TO CREATE A TRAFFIC VIRUS

When you submit articles you are in effect setting up valuable links with the submission website centres and every time you submit to a new centre you are gaining a new link. Additionally remember that the resource box in the articles contains your own website link. Tot it all up and what you have working for you is viral marketing and none of it is costing you anything but a little effort.

COMBINE LINKS WITH RESOURCES AND YOU'RE ON TO A WINNER

I had an astonishing experience recently which proves the validity of this statement. Read my web article below (reproduced on thousands of sites; driving hoards more traffic my way) and you'll see precisely what I mean.

Combine Links with Quality Resources and You're on a Winner

There are 1,001 ways to drive traffic to your websites.

I reckon I've tried most of them over the years and in the process have become blasé over the whole process of traffic promotion – but here's one that surprises even a hardened old cynic like me...

Several months ago I designed a single-page website, launched the creature as a sub-domain and promptly forgot about it. In point of fact it was so absentmindedly conceived that the tag still contains the template reference.

So what happened to it?

Here's what... it has achieved some amazing rankings.

- Yahoo! No. 2 (out of 8,270,000 web pages)
- AltaVista No. 2
- AllTheWeb No. 2

What's even better...

I attached my little afterthought single page to two of my prime sites and quality traffic is rocketing to both of them. These sites have always performed well for me but now they're on fire.

1st Creative Writing Course

No. 13 on Yahoo! (out of 8,270,000 web pages) for keyword phrase 'creative writing course'.

How To Products-XL

No. 10 on Yahoo! (Out of 706,000,000 – yes 706 million – web pages) for keyword phrase 'how to products'.

What is the secret of the single page winner?

It consists entirely of LINKS to QUALITY RESOURCES with reciprocal arrangements for most.

The trick is to narrow the focus on your niche and link to the cream of the marketplace including some of your competition...

If you visit the website in the resource box and click on RESOURCES you can check out my little one-page monster for yourself – and thereafter do a check on the search engines listed.

> Jim Green is a bestselling author with an ever-growing string of niche non-fiction titles to his credit. View his output at 1st-creative-writing-course.com.

And here is how the article looked in publication:

Fig. 13. Featured article in *Search Warp*.

26
What you should know about email marketing

Until comparatively recent times email was the favourite tool of most online marketers; that is until the 'spammers' moved in and ruined it for everyone. Well, *almost* ruined it. You can still use email to great effect if you go about matters correctly. Spam (the odious practice of sending email to thousands or even millions of people who have not requested it) is no longer tolerated. Nowadays offenders lose their local internet service provider, their websites, their email addresses, and more. Moreover, email server systems such as Yahoo! and Hotmail use highly sophisticated filters which weed out the bad boys and ban them outright.

- Don't even think about using bulk email; just one complaint (which you will get even if you try to hide) and your server will cancel your account.

BULK EMAIL V. OPT-IN EMAIL

And yet some reckless fruitcakes persist in bulk emailing even though they run the gauntlet every time they do it. Why do they persist? They look at it this way: although the response rates are extremely low, they still do manage to get a trickle of orders for their products and services – *meantime*, but not for long.

There is a better, legitimate way: opt-in email

Opt-in email works like this. You *invite* people to join your email list and you can do that in several acceptable ways.

- Through your website.

- Through subscriptions to your newsletter (which we'll cover in the next chapter).

- Through giving away free information produce.

All three of these options can operate in tandem. When visitors enter your site you capture their attention with an internal pop-up window or a carefully worded panel requesting them to subscribe to your newsletter. To qualify they must provide you with a current email address which gives you permission to contact them in future. Equally, to receive an e-book you give away for free, visitors must once again provide you with a legitimate email address and so you get the contact, they get the freebie; simple but highly effective and legal.

EXPOSING THE MYTHS ABOUT OPT-IN EMAIL

Many marketers never get around to implementing an opt-in email system because:

- **'I can't be bothered'** – You should; take the trouble to set up your own opt-in email system without delay. Email is free and when used correctly it leads to sales. If you elect not to participate you are leaving money on the table because by far the majority of online sales do not emanate directly from websites; they come from lists; lists of people who have given you permission to contact them; lists of people who have already purchased from you.

- **'I wouldn't know how'** – It's as simple as falling off a log when you employ the avenues listed above.

- **'I couldn't come up with content for a newsletter'** – Yes, you could. You have all the necessary material to hand in the articles you have already prepared and are continuing to write for distribution purposes. It just takes a little extra effort from you to set up and include them in your own newsletter.

- **'I won't be starting a newsletter; there are too many out there already'** – Oh, yes? Newsletters come and go, that's for sure, but the quality sheets go from strength to strength. If you don't fancy the standard format why not come up with something different? Like 'My Recipe for Today', 'My Marketing Tip for Today' or a newsletter in the form of an ongoing daily diary of how you are progressing your enterprise? What about a free online class? You could develop a six-, 12-, 24-lesson class on your topic and have subscribers receive the next issue every week, every two weeks, or once a month. Then, once they complete that class, you introduce advanced classes, etc. You could also put your subscribers on an updates list for new information constantly. Put your thinking cap on and create some ideas of your own before you ditch the notion of a newsletter.

- **'I don't see the point in giving stuff away for free'** – If you can't see the point, flick back to Chapter 23 for enlightenment.

TWELVE COMMON EMAIL MISTAKES TO AVOID

People make these mistakes all the time when using email and it costs them; they lose out on credibility. Don't allow that to happen to you and your retirement project.

1 – Omitting the subject line

Gone are the days when email users didn't realise the significance of the subject line. It makes no sense to send a message that reads 'No Subject' and seems to be about nothing of any consequence. Given the volume of email that everyone receives the subject header is essential if you want your message read. The subject line has become the hook.

2 – Not making the subject content meaningful

Your header should be pertinent to the message. The recipient is going to decide the order in which he/she reads emails based on who sent it and what it is about. Your virtual messages have lots of competition. If you want to interest recipients in a 'Great New Marketing Breakthrough', tell them so in the header.

3 – Failing to change the header to correspond with the subject

For example, if you are writing to your web publisher, your first header may be 'Website Content'. However, as your site develops and you send more information, label each message for what it is, 'Contact Info', 'Graphics', or 'Home Page'. Adding more details to the header will allow the recipient to find a specific document in his/her message folder without having to search every one you sent. Start a new message if you change the subject altogether.

4 – Failing to personalise the message

Email is informal but it still needs a greeting. Begin with 'Dear Mr. Broome', 'Dear Jim', 'Hello Jim', or just 'Jim'. Failure to insert the recipient's name can make you and your email seem cold.

5 – Not accounting for 'tone'

When you communicate with another person face to face, 93 per cent of the message is nonverbal. Email has no body language. The reader cannot see your face or hear your tone of voice, so chose your words carefully and thoughtfully. Put yourself in the other person's place and think how your words may come across in cyberspace.

6 – Forgetting to check for spelling and grammar

In the early days of email someone created the notion that this form of communication did not have to be letter perfect. Wrong. It does. It is a representation of you and your enterprise. If you don't check to be sure email is correct, people will question the calibre of other work you do.

Use proper capitalisation and punctuation, and always check your spelling. Remember that your spellchecker will catch misspelled words, but not misused ones. It cannot tell whether you meant to say 'from' or 'form', 'for' or 'fro', 'he' or 'the'.

7 – Composing an epic

Email is meant to be brief. Keep your message short. Use only a few paragraphs and a few sentences per paragraph. People skim, so a long missive is wasted. If you find yourself writing an overly long message, start editing down.

8 – Forwarding email without permission

If the message was sent to you and only you, why would you take responsibility for passing it on? Too often confidential information has gone global because of someone's lack of judgment. Unless you are asked, or request permission, do not forward anything that was sent just to you.

9 – Assuming that no one else will ever see your email

Once it has left your mailbox you have no idea where your email will end up. Don't use the internet to send anything that you couldn't stand to see on a local billboard. Use other means to communicate personal or sensitive information.

10 – Omitting your signature

Always close with your name, even though it is included at the top of the message and add contact information such as your phone, fax and street address. The recipient may want to call to talk further or send you documents that cannot be emailed. Creating a formal signature block with all that data is the most professional approach.

11 – Expecting an instant response

Not everyone is sitting in front of the computer with email turned on. The beauty of an internet communication is that it is convenient. It is not an interruption. People can check their messages when it suits them, not you. If your communication is so important that you need to hear back right away, use the phone.

12 – Completing the 'to' line first

The name or address of the person to whom you are writing is actually the last piece of information you should enter. Check everything else over carefully first; proof for grammar, punctuation, spelling and clarity. Did you say what needed to be said? How was your 'tone'? If you were the least bit emotional when you wrote the email, did you let it sit for a period of time? Did you include the attachment you wanted to send? If you enter the recipient's name first, a mere slip of the finger can send a message before its time. You can never take it back.

TWELVE MISTAKES THAT WILL SABOTAGE ANY EMAIL CAMPAIGN

1 – Don't load the copy, push 'send' and move on

We've all got a lot on our plates and it's easy to be trigger-happy with the send button. Have you received emails with misspellings or odd formatting? It makes you think twice about the sender.

Take time to proof your emails before they go out. Run a spellchecker, and make sure the format looks the way you expected it to in the top email clients (e.g., AOL, Outlook, Eudora). Also, review list selection and verify any personalisation rules.

2 – Don't include lots of broken links

Broken links are a major cause of reduced response. A study by email marketing software and services firm Silverpop found nearly half of all emails contain errors such as broken graphics or raw HTML code. Even when earlier versions of AOL and Lotus Notes (which has always been problematic) are eliminated from results, more than 18 per cent of HTML emails had some rendering problem.

Set up test accounts with the major online services and see for yourself how your campaigns display.

3 – Don't ignore spam filters

The deliverability maze can be so overwhelming that it's tempting to just ignore the topic. If your messages don't get through they can't drive revenue. Use a content checker to scan your subject line and body copy to improve the odds that your mail won't be filtered out. Most email service bureaus offer built-in content checkers. Plus, there also are free online resources to test your message before it goes out. This is the content checker I use:

http://spamcheck.sitesell.com

Submit test versions of your email, and this service will provide a free evaluation of your campaign and indicate what might trigger a filter.

4 – Don't ignore your bounces

Today's internet service providers (ISPs) are very demanding and one area of focus is undeliverable email coming from individual marketers. If you exceed their standards for undeliverable or bounced messages, they may flag you as a spammer and your mail may be blocked.

There's some good news on this front. Email marketing and online advertising firm DoubleClick has done an excellent job at monitoring quarterly trends and publishing the results on its site. The firm's latest report shows bounce rates across its client base have declined to 11.5 percent. But that's still high!

Establish thresholds for re-mailing both hard and soft bounces and retire email addresses after threshold limits are exceeded.

5 – Don't capture several pages of data during registration

Direct marketers are data junkies and it's tempting to want to know everything possible about online registrants. Have you ever been intrigued by an offer, yet abandoned the sign-up process when you were asked too many questions?

6 – Don't design an email plan without looking at the website

An email recipient may click on a beautifully crafted email and be brought to a landing page or micro site that has a totally different look and feel. This is especially true if you're doing affiliate work. Remember the best user experience is a seamless one. Your emails should be consistent with the site you're promoting.

Short registration forms work, and you can still ask qualifying questions. Make it easy to complete, and don't ask for information you're not going to use. An important statistic to examine is the abandonment rate for your sign-up forms.

7 – Don't select rental email lists based on price

There are inexpensive cost-per-action (CPA) lists available. Marketers pay only for those recipients who meet performance criteria set in advance: clicks, registrations or purchases. On the surface this sounds like a great deal: you control your marketing costs and pay only if someone responds. Be wary though. Many CPA lists simply blast all names on the list rather than use selection criteria. Also, the level of permission may be suspect. Use these lists and you run the risk of being labeled a spammer.

Work with a quality e-list broker who provides information such as prior usage and how the individuals opted in. Expect that most good lists will only be available on a cost-per-thousand basis.

8 – Don't keep your list size up by making it hard to opt out

Some marketers ask you to reply to a message and include 'remove me' or 'unsubscribe' in the subject line. The theory behind this is that more people will stay on the list. But this practice reduces the effectiveness of the list. Communicate with recipients who welcome your message and you will have better results.

9 – Don't sell, sell, sell …

E-commerce marketers want to monetise their efforts by selling goods and services. It's tempting to fill every inch of your emails with product offerings.

The best email plans have a balance between selling and content. The content can provide behind-the-scenes information about products, tell a story about your company, or provide tips and hints on how customers use a product.

Value-added content will keep your recipients interested. A great example of this is the Lands' End newsletter. The lead article is always a long-form article that sometimes sells but often presents a story about what's happening in Dodgeville, WI, or a customer testimonial about a product. The copy is impeccable, and I suspect their open rates are much higher than average.

10 – Don't think online only

The beauty of email is that it's a great way to promote your offer and drive traffic right to your content. However, customers or prospects may not want to order online. Don't think only in one dimension.

Provide ways for recipients to contact you offline by including your toll-free number both in emails and on your site. Some marketers have measured the impact of including their 0800 number in emails and found up to 20 per cent of sales came in through the call centre.

One interesting twist on offering a contact option is eStara's Push to Talk technology that can be implemented either in an email or on a website. Once the recipient clicks the Push to Talk link, he or she is prompted to enter a phone number and a time for a return call from a sales or customer service agent. This information is routed automatically to your call centre.

11 – Don't forget to make time to test or measure

Testing and analysis take time and time always seems to be in short supply. If you approach each email as a one-time event that lives or dies based on results, you never will achieve all that you could.

A plan with specific goals will provide you with a road map to success. Testing is relatively easy in email. Create hypotheses and test to see if you're right. Build upon your previous efforts in terms of what worked and what didn't work. Your campaigns should be interconnected.

12 – Don't assume offline customers would have registered if they wanted to receive emails

This may be true for a percentage of your customers but there are many who simply haven't thought to sign up. Email appending works for many marketers who want to farther penetrate their customer database. Select a quality supplier with a database that clearly is permission-based. Take the time to nurture any names with a special plan.

Obviously, no one would deliberately sabotage an email campaign. Consider this food for thought to help maximise your efforts.

FIVE WAYS TO EARN MORE USING EMAIL

Use this short checklist to ensure that you are taking full advantage of the power of email and by so doing, making time your ally, not your adversary. Fast, easy, and free, the consistent use of email in the following areas will yield powerful results for you.

1 – Customer follow-up

Whether it's as simple as a one-time 'thank you' or as elaborate as a 50-message follow up system, customers love to know you care. As a minimum, send one message thanking customers for every order.

2 – Customer learning

Do you offer a product that takes a bit of learning to use? Teach your customers how to get the benefits they deserve from your product or service via email.

Keep messages on topic and separate your follow up series into bite-size learning pieces. These follow up messages can bring your refund rate to near zero.

3 – Pre-sales series

How often do *you* buy the first thing you see? Comparison shopping is the way of the internet and getting prospective customers to return to your site is the challenge. A pre-sale series is the answer and it's very easy to do. Just write down the top ten reasons why someone should buy from you, then put each in a follow up message. Send one a day until they are all delivered. Offer the series to everyone who visits your site and let time do the selling work for you. My experience has been that up to 40 per cent of visitors will take your free information if you do a good job of selling the idea.

4 – Special pricing and offers

Use email to deliver insider information on special bargains, limited time pricing, and more. Much like a coupon sheet in your local newspaper, selling advertising in this type of email is a breeze.

5 – Hard-to-find news

People love offbeat news, especially when it has a connection to their lives.

For an example of this technique visit this website (you'll love it!):

www.thisistrue.com.

More ideas about how to use email to sell more could include:

1. Announce special events.

2. Do a joint venture (JV) with someone whose product compliments your own.

3. Sell a message in your follow up series.

4. Teach affiliates how to sell more for you.

5. Create a discussion to do research for your next product.

Email makes everything easier and faster, creating a powerful commercial impression and establishing positive professional relationships. The retiree entrepreneur who uses the technology effectively and appropriately will see the results of that effort reflected in the bottom line.

27
Why you should create your own newsletter

So, you've decided to start a newsletter focused on your profitable retirement pursuit? I'm glad to hear it. You are about to embark on a very exciting and rewarding venture – watching your online publication grow, trying out new tactics to attract subscribers, even making some money. It becomes addictive. You'll see why as you progress.

COMMON GOALS ALL NEWSLETTER PUBLISHERS SHARE

All newsletter publishers want:

- Increased subscriptions.
- Increased exposure.

Driving subscriptions and enhancing the profile of your newsletter are the core activities for success. There are 300,000+ other newsletters competing for the same subscribers, so the better you become at chasing your goals, the faster you will succeed. Gaining momentum is the hardest part. Where do you begin in your quest for say, 10,000 subscribers and maximum exposure?

Key No. 1: submit to newsletter directories

Before you jump in though: have another look at the description you have created for your newsletter. With so many ezines already out there, what is going to make yours stand out from the rest?

If anyone were to look at 100+ titles in your category, why would they choose yours?

Your description is a key element to attracting new subscribers and so it's a good practice to study other ezine descriptions before creating your own. Visit a few of the top directories and search through various newsletters in the same category as your own.

Here are a few websites to get you started:
www.ezineaction.com
www.ezineadvertising.com
www.ezine-dir.com
www.ezinelocater.com
www.ezine-marketing.com
www.ezinesearch.com
www.ezinestoday.com
www.ezinearticles.com
www.new-list.com

Take note of which descriptions catch your eye. Which jump out at you? Which are as dull as ditch water? www.e-zines.com is a great site to get up to speed on writing good descriptions.

Here's an example of a good description ...

> Powerful internet marketing concepts that you can use right now; informative articles written by professional marketers who make their living online, money making tips and tricks you must use to increase your profits, and much more! Receive four free gifts when you subscribe!

Here's an example of a poor description ...

> An electronic newsletter especially created to help new and/or frustrated internet marketers prosperously market online.

See the difference? They're both internet marketing newsletters. Which one would you subscribe to?

Once you have studied competitive descriptions, develop a few of your own. Then pick the best one.

Another incentive to submit your newsletter to the directories

In a concerted effort to increase search engine ranking most of these directories submit their website on a regular basis. And guess what? Your newsletter title will also start showing up in the major engines – increasing exposure even further.

Key No. 2: announce your ezine through announcement lists

Announcement lists are extremely powerful. When used correctly they have the potential to bring in 500–700 subscribers in a single week. What are announcement lists? They are mailing lists that are dedicated to announcing new newsletters on a daily or weekly basis. Most of them will allow you to announce your ezine including your description and subscription information.

Here's a short list to get you started:

List Builder: List_Builder-subscribe@topica.com
1 List Advertising: www.groups.yahoo.com
A Announce: www.groups.yahoo.com
Add Your List: www.groups.yahoo.com

Key No. 3: use the power of free ads

Using free ads is nothing new, but don't underestimate them; they constitute a powerful tool to have in your marketing arsenal. There are two basic types: free and swaps. How do swaps work? It's pretty obvious. You contact ezine publishers and approach them about exchanging ads. There's a catch with free ads – most of them include other people's ads and as a result are not as potent as swaps. You'll need an auto-responder for both types and here are some suggestions:

www.aweber.com
www.getresponse.com

www.autobots.net
www.autoresponders.com
www.freeautobot.com
www.ultimateresponse.com

You don't need to waste time submitting your ads manually. Here's a piece of software that lets you blast out hundreds of free ads and ad swap requests with a few clicks of your mouse. It also includes over 275 ad swap sources and 100+ free ad sources with tracking capabilities built into the software.

To download a trial version, visit this website:

www.articleannouncer.com/

Key No. 4: let your articles auto-promote your ezine

Writing articles for other ezines may be the most effective and easiest way to market your newsletter. In fact, some successful publishers use articles as their only source of promotion. You already know the drill. You learned it in Chapter 24.

The *Article Announcer* software link immediately above is an inexpensive way of handling distribution.

Key No. 5: exchange links with similar ezines/websites

Here's a little story I heard recently; and it's true.

A group of local fast-food restaurant owners were complaining about the lack of business. One of them had a bizarre idea. He approached three of his competitors and asked whether they would promote his restaurant if he did the same for theirs. The fish & chip, pizza, and burger restaurants all began to promote each other. Guess what happened? Everyone's business increased.

This technique will also work for you when you link to other related newsletters and websites.

TWO SECRETS THAT CONVERT YOUR EZINE INTO A CASH MACHINE

Secret 1: your subscriber list is everything to you

Your emailing list is central to everything connected with your online activity. It needs to be made up of good quality recipients and, ideally, it needs to be quite big. Most important of all, you must take the time and trouble to look after the subscribers who have bothered to sign up.

Let me give you a couple of examples:

1. **Make plain your publishing intention and stick to it.** If you advertise that you intend to send out your newsletter on a Wednesday, stick with that schedule. Random editions sent when your recipients are least expecting them might make them think that you are running a slap-dash venture. If they think that your offerings are less than professional then they'll probably migrate to one of your competitors.

2. **Never endorse a product you haven't tried or don't like.** You want to make money from your newsletter and that's good. But make sure that you are providing your readers with pure quality. Resist the ever-present temptation to recommend and endorse a product simply because the vendor is running an affiliate program paying you out a high percentage of the sale proceeds. You might make a few extra pounds in the short term, but it'll cost you subscribers (that's money too) in the longer run by destroying trust between you and your readers.

So treat your readers like kings and queens. Never abuse their trust and work to build their loyalty. Remember: your subscriber list is everything to you.

Secret 2: brainstorming for the perfect newsletter topic

First of all you must acknowledge that the list of possible newsletter topics is virtually endless. You don't need to be the editor of yet another publication spouting on about how to make money on the internet. That is what almost everyone else does. Try brainstorming to uncover an offbeat, wacky topic. For instance, would you consider producing a newsletter that sends jokes to its readers on a daily basis? You wouldn't make money from it, right? Wrong. Someone does. His name is Ray Owens. He set up the 'Joke-A-Day' ezine and is reported to have pulled in £85,000 revenue in the process through selling advertising and merchandise in the past year alone.

The key advantage of an online newsletter over conventional publishing is the ability to speak to a tiny niche section, even just a sub-section of an interested group of people.

TIP

The *Easy Ezine Toolkit* spells out how to brainstorm for the perfect money-making newsletter topic and how to test market your shortlist to discover which subject will bring you the most subscribers flooding in. If that sounds good to you, head over to www.howtocorp.com/sales.php?offer=writing333&pid=6 now and get instant access to the web's best ezine creator toolkit. I use it – and so should you if you want your newsletter to be both original and successful.

"Discover The Secrets Behind The Web's Most Successful Ezine Newsletters"

This Toolkit Provides You With The Proven Trade Secrets To Build Your Own Incredibly Successful Ezine Publication.

From the desk
of Michael Green
Friday August 27, 2004

"I'd been messing around with getting an Ezine together and had even put a couple of issues out, but I wasn't really getting much response. Then I stumbled across your Easy Ezine Toolkit and thought: 'Hey, I'll give it a go'. Your eBook manual was easy to follow and simply by cutting-and-pasting the Ezine templates you supplied I was

Fig. 14. *Easy Ezine Toolkit.*

28
The power of list building to assemble a bank of prospects

There's a frequently-quoted saying among successful e-entrepreneurs, '*The money is in the list*'. And so it is. More sales are generated from quality lists than from any other online marketing activity. Build a list of targeted contacts for your profitable retirement pursuit – and sales will follow. I can't think of anyone better to convince you of the power of building an opt-in list than my online friend Shelley Lowery. Shelley is a hands-on expert and her own list at web-source.net is well into six figures. She recently produced a cutting edge article on the subject and has kindly given me permission to reproduce it here.

SECRETS TO BUILDING MASSIVE OPT-IN LISTS

An opt-in list is the absolute most effective marketing tool available on the internet. Not only does it provide you with a direct line of communication with your target market, it also enables you to develop a trusting relationship with your subscribers.

The key to using an opt-in list effectively is to develop a large subscriber base. If you've struggled with increasing your subscriber base this article will reveal some of the most effective methods used to build an opt-in list. If you're not using these methods you're losing hundreds of new subscribers each week.

If you really want to build a massive list you must provide your potential subscribers with an incentive. Competition on the internet is fierce. You can no longer simply tell visitors what your publication will provide and expect a large percentage to subscribe. It simply won't work.

There are thousands of publications online and most of your visitors are probably already subscribed to many. Why would they want to subscribe to another one? Sure, you'll get some new subscribers, but how many? Enough to build a massive opt-in list? The truth is, if you continue to build your list simply by displaying a sign-up box on your site and listing your publication at the listing sites it will take years to develop a substantial list. You *must* give your visitors a reason to subscribe.

Incentives

Using incentives is a highly effective method of obtaining new subscribers. However, they must be of value and of interest to your target audience.

Some popular incentives include:

• Exclusive e-books that provide valuable information that will be of interest to your target market.

• Special reports that provide exclusive, detailed information in regard to a specific subject.

• Special software programs that will assist your visitors.

If you're not comfortable developing your own incentives there are hundreds of great e-books available online that you may freely distribute. You can find some here: www.web-source.net/free_ebooks.htm.

Subscription exchange incentives

In addition to using incentives to gain new subscribers you can also use a subscription exchange. In exchange for your visitor's subscription, you could provide any of the following:

• Provide access to a 'members only' area of your website.

• Provide a service.

• List their website within your directory or integral search engine.

In order for your visitors to use your services they agree to receive your publication.

Popup windows

Although popup windows can be irritating if not used correctly they provide a highly effective means of obtaining new subscribers. The key to using popup windows effectively is to combine them with your incentives.

Design a small popup window that utilises 'cookies' and only displays the first time your visitor enters your site. This window should contain information about your publication and incentive. It might read something like this:

'Subscribe to A1 Marketing Tips and receive a copy of the highly acclaimed e-book, *Secrets of the Internet Marketing Gurus* completely free.'

Your subscription box should follow this sentence.

You can find a nice popup script that utilises cookies here:

www.web-source.net/javascript_popup_window3.htm

You can find a complete list of sites offering free scripts here:

www.web-source.net/web/JavaScripts/

Alert boxes

Although using popup windows with incentives is a highly effective method of obtaining new subscribers there is one other method that is even better. When combined with an incentive this method will literally double your subscriptions instantly. It's similar to a popup window but it doesn't require your visitor to fill out a form.

When a visitor enters your site an alert box will appear. This alert box should display text requesting their subscription and information about your incentive. Your visitor can choose to click on 'OK' to subscribe or 'Cancel' to close the alert.

The alert box is displayed via a script that extracts your visitor's name and email address. If they choose to subscribe it then sends their subscription request, via email, to your subscription address and adds it to your database. In addition, you can send personalised messages to your subscribers; use auto-responder follow-ups and provide your subscribers with 'one click' unsubscribe links within your messages.

To increase your subscriptions even further you can also place a subscription box on each page of your website.

For further information, visit:

www.web-source.net/

Conclusion

No matter how many new subscribers you may acquire, the key to a successful opt-in list is keeping them. The relationship you build with your subscribers will determine your success. Above all, you must provide your readers with quality content. They subscribed to your publication for a reason. If it doesn't meet their expectations they'll simply unsubscribe.

Once you've developed a trusting relationship with your subscribers, your personal recommendations will be a very effective method of closing sales. However, it is very important that you only recommend a product or service that you truly believe in. Your professional reputation depends on it.

Copyright © Shelley Lowery

www.web-source.net

Shelley Lowery is the author of the acclaimed web design course *Web Design Mastery* www.webdesignmastery.com and e-book Starter – *Give Your Ebooks the Look and Feel of a Real Book* www.ebookstarter.com. Visit Web-Source.net to sign up for a complimentary subscription to Etips and receive a copy of the acclaimed e-book *Killer Internet Marketing Strategies*.

I have personally learned more from Shelley Lowery on the subject of opt-in list building than from any other leading online marketer. She has helped enormously in my own quest for a profitable retirement pursuit.

29
Converting prospects into customers

You have come a long way in the development of your online retirement pursuit, but to make it profitable your focus must always be on converting prospects into cash-paying customers. Mastering the basics – creating ideas, turning them into produce, and learning how to promote isn't enough. These are just the tools to get you moving. Now you must drive the engine. Let's look at the buying process from the flipside: why prospects *won't* buy from you when you fail to appreciate the rules of converting them into customers.

TEN REASONS WHY PEOPLE WON'T BUY FROM YOU

Here are 10 simple yet powerful ideas for you to reflect on. They will help you adjust your marketing strategies on everything you sell.

1 – You don't make people feel safe when they order

Remind people that they are ordering through a secure server. Tell them you won't sell their email address and all their information will be kept confidential.

2 – You don't make your ad copy attractive

Your ad lists features instead of benefits. The headline does not attract your target audience. You don't list any testimonials or guarantees in your ad.

257

3 – You don't remind people to come back and visit

People usually don't purchase the first time they visit. The more times they visit your site, the greater the chance they will buy. The most effective way is to give them a free subscription to your newsletter.

4 – You don't let people know anything about your business

They will feel more comfortable if they know who they are buying from. Publish a section entitled 'About Us' on your website. Include your profile, contact information, etc.

5 – You don't give people as many ordering options as possible

Accept credit cards, cheques, money orders, and other forms of electronic payments. Take orders by phone, email, website, fax, mail, etc.

6 – You don't make your website look professional

You must have your own domain name. Your website should be easy to navigate through. The graphics should be related to the theme of your site.

7 – You don't let people read your ad before they get your freebie

When you use free stuff to lure people to your website include the reference *below* your ad copy or on another web page. If you list the freebie above your ad they may never look to see what you're selling.

8 – You don't attract the target audience that would buy your product or service

A simple way to check on this is to survey your existing customers to see what attracted them to buy. This information will help you improve your target marketing and advertising.

9 – You don't test and improve your ad copy

Many people never change their ad copy. You have to test frequently and improve to get the highest possible response rate.

10 – You don't give people any urgency to buy

Some prospects are interested in your product, but they are put off buying it till later and eventually forget about it. Entice them to buy now with a freebie or discount and include a deadline date when the offer ends.

THE GOLDEN RULE OF SELLING

You will never *actually sell* anything to anyone at any time – but they might just buy from you …

1. If you are operating in the same marketplace as your prospects.

2. If you respect their intelligence.

3. If you are honest with them.

4. If you give them good reason to trust you.

5. If you know what it is they want.

6. If you can provide a genuine solution.

7. If your produce does all you say it will do.

8. If you can back up your claims with unsolicited testimonials

9. If you can offer a guarantee.

10. If you make it easy for your prospects to pay you.

Cautionary note: complete compliance with points 2–10 won't amount to a row of beans if you miss the target on Point No. 1. Shout as hard and as long as you want in the marketplace but make sure it's the right marketplace.

30
How to accept credit card payments

If you don't accept credit cards at your website you will not get many sales. However, before we launch into a review of credit card processing systems it is worth noting that despite growing universal usage there is still uneasiness among consumers about disclosing credit card details online. The following extract from a survey published in March 2004 highlights this concern.

CONSUMER FEARS ON DISCLOSING CREDIT CARD INFORMATION

More than 50 per cent of consumers recently surveyed by Jupiter Research Incorporated fear the personal information supplied in an online transaction will be sold to a retailer's marketing partners and generate unwanted marketing messages. More than a third of those surveyed also expressed concerns that unauthorised recurring transactions, such as subscription renewals, could result from supplying credit card information online. In the survey,

- 30 per cent of consumers worried about merchants not shipping products for which their credit card had been charged online;

- 20 per cent worried that a merchant could debit a card number supplied online for a higher price than the advertised price.

Older consumers were more concerned with identity theft – 63 per cent of those over age 55 surveyed saw it as a threat versus 56 per cent of those aged 18 to 14. Identity theft concerns lessened as consumers' online tenure increased. Among young and less-tenured consumers the greatest concern was merchant duplicity. For example, 32 per cent of those surveyed aged 18 to 24 expressed concern about being charged more than they agreed to pay at checkout versus 20 per cent of survey respondents overall.

Confidence that technology solutions such as Verified by Visa could prevent fraud increased as online tenure increased. Significantly, Jupiter notes that 'newbies' (defined as those with only limited online tenure) will constitute a smaller portion of the overall online audience in years to come. As newbies will comprise a significantly lower percentage of the population moving forward it is necessary to present messages that focus increasingly on a tenured online population.

Bear in mind that this survey relates mainly to the North American market where online users are more attuned to purchasing by credit cards. A similar study for the UK where users are less attuned and even more cautious might paint a bleaker picture. Even so, you need to accept credit card payments, and to assist you in selecting a system compatible with your requirements here is a review of seven leading processors.

Website	PayPal (paypal.co.uk)
Setup/Monthly Fees	No/No
Orders By	Online Only
Locations	International with USA-bias
Processing Fees	Credit cards, 2.2% + 30 cents, no minimum Non-credit card, 1.6% + 30 cents
Extras	Payment to you is made into your bank account, or onto your credit card. Payments under $15 are only charged 30 cents.
Notes	Americans can use Web-Accept (accept credit card orders on their websites). International accounts can be opened, but are not able to use Web-Accept yet, although you can be paid by other PayPal users. Fee for $10 item 30 cents Fee for $100 item 250 cents Overall Cheapest Fees. A great service, cheaper than a merchant account.

Website	Verza Inc. (verza.com)
Setup/Monthly Fees	No/No
Orders By	Online Only
Locations	International
Processing Fees	Credit cards, 99 cents + 4.9%, Cheques 99 cents + 3.5%.
Extras	Payments twice per month. 5% six-month rolling-reserve. Additional $15 for each chargeback. Includes an account control centre to view your account details and transaction logs.
Notes	Fee for $10 item 148 cents Fee for $100 item 589 cents

Website	Verotel (verotel.com)
Setup/Monthly Fees	No/No
Orders By	Cheques, credit cards and 1-900 number billing.
Locations	International
Processing Fees	Depends on transaction type and ticket price.
Extras	10% rolling reserve. $15 for each chargeback.
Notes	Credit card processing limited to **content**. Highly flexible service with several extras such as 'set up your own reseller programme free', 'real time control centre' and '1-900 billing'. Fee for $10 item 150 cents Fee for $75 (max by credit card) item 900 cents

Website	Internet Billing Company (ibill.com)
Setup/Monthly Fees	No/No
Orders By	Online
Locations	USA
Processing Fees	15% for up to $10,000 in sales per billing period. Graded reductions for increases in volume.
Extras	10% 6-month rolling reserve.
Notes	Limited to sales of access, content or services. Apparently, in order to use real time delivery with iBill, you need some custom CGI scripts. Fee for $10 item 150 cents Fee for $100 item 1500 cents

Website	Shareit (shareit.com)
Setup/Monthly Fees	No/No
Orders By	Online, Phone, Fax, Mail
Locations	USA + Germany
Processing Fees	$2.95 + 4%
Extras	Mailing a cheque = $5, issuing bank also deducts $5. Alternatively you can have payment wire transferred to your account. Cheques issued once per month.
Notes	They originally set out to act as a third party for shareware writers, but will accept credit card orders for any product or service. Based in Germany, are good for Europeans and allow you to accept the Euro as payment. Fee for $10 item 335 cents Fee for $100 item 695 cents

Website	CC Now (ccnow.com)
Setup/Monthly Fees	No/No
Orders By	Online
Locations	International
Processing Fees	9% (8% in Nov/Dec)
Extras	Reserve if your monthly volume is $1000+
Notes	Limited to sales of physical goods. Fee for $10 item 95 cents Fee for $100 item 950 cents

Website	Clickbank (clickbank.com)
Setup/Monthly Fees	$49.95/No
Orders By	Online
Locations	International
Processing Fees	$1.50 + 7.5%
Extras	No-longer free! Only issue cheques, and only if over $25. Charge $2.50 to process and send cheque. Withhold 10% of cheques over $25 which is released after approx 90 days. Cheques issued twice per month.
Notes	Service is limited to authors of unique internet content and services. If you distribute your own original information via web pages, files, or email, then ClickBank is ideal for you. You have the option to recruit resellers for your products, all details handled by Clickbank. You can also refer people to Clickbank and earn money if anyone you send to Clickbank signs up and makes sales. Not for sale of physical goods, recurring billing or with shopping carts. Fee for $10 item 225 cents Fee for $100 item 900 cents

PERSONAL PREFERENCES

Of these options I personally feel more comfortable using the first and last: Paypal and Clickbank. They are reliable, ultra security conscious, provide excellent account facilities, and always pay out on the due date.

ClickBank offers a magnificent service and I've always used it as my prime payment processor. It's fast, efficient, and above all, universally accepted. However, if you promote a multitude of digital products it has one much-heralded drawback. Either:

1. You are required to fork out another $49 every time you introduce a new creation on a disparate location, or …

2. You are required to host all of your merchandise on **one** website.

Not any more; at least certainly not for me. You see, I have developed a safe, legitimate method of selling all of my ever-growing produce using ClickBank on a single fee of $49.

You can learn more about my secret system at this website:

howtoproducts-xl.com/ccc.html.

31

How to point-and-click your way to retirement profits

This is the final lesson in how to promote your profitable retirement opportunity and it's an important one. You have everything in position: niche market, niche produce, niche marketing strategy. All you need now is a few automated tools to help you point and click your way to retirement profits.

So far we have managed to contain start-up costs to the bare minimum but to expedite progress, here is where it will pay you in the long run to invest a little money before you launch headlong into your prescribed marketplace. I could provide you with a gigantic list of tools and just let you get on with the matter of selection by yourself. Instead I am going to suggest you give serious consideration to just two pieces of software that work for me and will do an equally good job for you.

MARLON SANDERS' *MARKETING DASHBOARD*

This is a unique piece of software (I've never seen anything else like it) that enables you to house everything you will use to market your produce in one convenient location in your computer. Marlon calls it point-and-click marketing and I reckon it is destined to become one of the cornerstones of online promotion. You just click on the icons on the dashboard and save yourself endless hours sifting through thousands of pages of data.

Fig. 15. Marlon Sanders' *Marketing Dashboard*.

This is what the software does for you:

1. **Walks you step-by-step** through setting up your system without requiring you to wade through reams of information that takes time to read, decipher, analyse and apply.

2. **Simplifies your marketing**. All you do is click and follow the instructions. You don't have to try to figure out what's next. You just click the next icon and follow the steps.

3. **Takes away the confusion**. Every step is clearly laid out and labelled with big, blue numbers. You don't have to try to interpret how XYZ method applies to your individual situation.

4. **Gives you an A to Z system**. Everything is covered from your marketing vision, to your profit plan, to your break even point, to your merchant account, shopping cart, domain name selection, stats tracking, ftp, backing up your files, speed researching, organising your tasks and information – and much more. You won't find anything else like it anywhere. No stone is left unturned.

5. **Eases promotion** because it is designed for beginners. Marlon's

purpose in creating the program is to make it easy for beginners to master online promotion.

6. **Increases your confidence**. The entire program is based on the creator's experience in online marketing since before the web existed, so you can depend on it to increase your own confidence as you find your way around cyberspace promotion.

7. **Visually demonstrates what to do with screen captures**. Included are numerous screen captures to demonstrate individual steps, without overwhelming you with needless details or endless dialogue. Marlon has struck a balance to make this simple, practical and useable.

8. **Offers you free trials** of innovative, new software programs that speed and simplify your marketing.

What does the Marketing Dashboard cost? Just a one-time payment of $59.95 (approx. £33) and you can access it on a 30-day free trial before you buy at this website: www.getitgoing.com/.

MICHAEL GREEN'S *HOW TO PROMOTE A PRODUCT*

I've known Michael Green (no relation!) for some time. He is the only world class online marketer residing in the United Kingdom and is highly respected by his peers around the world. Michael heads up a long established and successful offline print business, but his consuming passion is online marketing in the shape of the 20 niche products he distributes through his How To Corp.com.

In this book you have learned the basics on online promotion for your profitable retirement pursuit but you will go into overdrive if you invest in Michael Green's *How to Promote a Product*. I use it daily and it has taught me a great deal (as has Michael himself).

Here are the bare bones of his book:

• 24 Power Keys that work whether you are an experienced marketer or a complete newcomer to internet marketing.

- 24 Power Keys that work whether you are promoting a product or a service.

- 24 Power Keys that work no matter what it is that you are trying to sell online.

And the benefits:

- Turn your existing product into a super hot top-seller on the net. Michael provides you with the exact formula that he uses personally. Follow it to the letter and he virtually guarantees that your product will quickly become an online sensation.

- Instantly rejuvenate your flagging online sales by discovering how to promote your product using the 24 secret Power Keys. If you've got a product, but it isn't selling so well, then *How to Promote a Product* will pick it up by its bootstraps and yank it back right where it belongs – selling day and night – and putting cash back in your bank account.

- Use it to launch your new products (or services) and turn them into overnight successes. This toolkit will work for you whether you've got an existing product or you need to start promoting your brand new soon-to-be-launched product or service.

- Take someone else's product and promote it like there's no tomorrow. You can use every one of these tools to market someone else's product as an affiliate marketer. In fact you'll probably end up making more cash than the owner.

- Tailored for newcomers marketing their first product or someone else's. Now there's no need to allow inexperience of the internet marketing world prevent you from clocking up stunning sales. Just follow the system Michael has laid out for you in easy-to-follow black and white.

- These 24 proven Power Keys to promoting your product apply to you no matter what you are selling online. That's right. You could be selling cod liver oil, widgets or an internet marketing product. All that matters is that you're setting out to promote your product online.

- Supercharge your sales. Why settle for selling your product now and then when it could be selling like hotcakes every day? If your product isn't selling as well as you'd like it's nothing to do with the product itself and everything to do with the way that you're currently promoting it online.

How to Promote a Product costs $149 (approx. £83) but you will recoup the cost in a matter of weeks if you follow the guidelines. Available for purchase and download at:

www.howtocorp.com/sales.php?offer=writing333&pid=22

32
What will the future hold for online trading?

Online trading is here to stay, that's for sure. It won't go away and it can only go from strength to strength. But in which diverse directions will it expand? And how can we get a glimpse of the future and what it holds for online marketing? How do you find out if what works today will cut the mustard a year or so from now? Where can we find answers to these and other vital questions? One expert claims to have the key to up and coming events. He built a website around the issue and created a comprehensive course: *378 Internet Marketing Predictions* – a foretaste of which you can gain access to at the end of this chapter. It is worth a look. Some of the notions expressed might seem crackpot on the first reading but then you never know.

Some very famous people got it all wrong when making predictions about innovation, so maybe the creator of this website and the course knows something the gurus don't or are unwilling to face up to.

WHAT SOME FAMOUS PEOPLE HAD TO SAY ABOUT INNOVATION

'Who the hell wants to hear actors talk?' Harry Warner, Warner Brothers Pictures, 1927.

'I think there's a world market for about 5 computers.' Thomas Watson, chairman of IBM, 1943.

'Man will never reach the moon regardless of all future scientific advances.' Dr. Lee De Forest, 1939.

'Heavier-than-air flying machines are impossible.' Lord Kelvin, president, Royal Society, 1895.

'There is no reason anyone would want a computer in their home.' Ken Olson, president, chairman and founder of Digital Equipment Corp 1977.

'640k ought to be enough for anybody.' Bill Gates, 1981.

TWENTY-NINE QUESTIONS RAISED IN *378 INTERNET MARKETING PREDICTIONS*

1. Which search engine is going to beat Google and Yahoo?

2. What new form of advertising is going to sweep the online world?

3. How will interactive agents make their way to internet marketing?

4. How will virtual reality and artificial intelligence revolutionise the online world in 2005–2006?

5. What impact will new/emerging technologies have on internet marketing, especially affiliate marketing?

6. What's going to happen to email publishing?

7. What new/innovative promotion and branding tools are emerging?

8. What's in stock for online multimedia?

9. What is the hottest forecasted resell rights markets?

10. In what new and innovative ways will internet marketers target?

11. What factors are going to reshuffle the rankings of internet marketers?

12. Which advertising and promotion methods are bearish and why?

13. Who's developing pop over/hover ad blockers?

14. What is the strongest, ever-bullish trend in online advertising?

15. What new advertising and promotion methods are bullish?

16. What is the 'magnet' that's going to attract online advertising dollars?

17. What's 'Chameleon' advertising? Is it bullish or bearish? How can you use it?

18. Which form of advertising is going to be the successor of contextual advertising?

19. What new form of advertising is going to sweep the online world, producing the best responses, generating the highest click-throughs and maximum revenues?

20. What's about to become the coolest, most innovative 'medium' for advertising, and one of the most powerful 'branding' tools? Some companies like Coca Cola, Sony Ericsson, Puma, Nokia to name a few have already started using it.

21. How will advertising become more interactive?

22. What new online places will businesses advertise in?

23. What will advertising evolve to?

24. What about ad tracking and the importance of tracking?

25. How will multimedia conquer the web?

26. What impact will multimedia have on internet marketing, online publishing, resell rights marketing, advertising and promotion?

27. What multimedia solution is Armand Morin working on together with VoxWire?

28. What two technologies are going to team up to make the delivery of big-sized, full-blown multimedia 'newsletters' a matter of minutes rather than hours?

29. How will streaming multimedia impact different industries and markets, and revolutionise the way information is presented online?

Go on, have a peek into the future ... it won't hurt.

www.internet-marketing-predictions.com/

33
Checklist for getting
it all together

We have reached the end of our journey on the formation of your retirement money-maker plan and in particular its relevance to online venturing. In a nutshell: it's all about joined-up marketing; how everything you do is joined together. There are no random events; none whatever. One act leads to another in the logical progression for success and *if you don't understand this one simple but vital point* your enterprise will stutter and stumble until it grinds to a halt.

So, to help you ensure that in respect of your retirement money-making plan you really have got it all together, I conclude with a list of questions which this book should have enabled you to answer. If you can't remember, then the page references will help you to refresh your memory.

CHOOSING A PROFITABLE PURSUIT IN RETIREMENT

- Do you now fully appreciate what this will entail?
- Do you understand the implications of entrepreneurship in the third age?
- What are the advantages?
- What are the drawbacks?
- What's on offer for the enterprising retiree?

(Pages 3 to 8)

PUTTING YOUR LIFETIME KNOWLEDGE TO WORK

- Could you write a book using your know-how?

- What would you need to do to bring it to fruition?

- Have you given thought to an electronic version?

- How would you adapt your expertise for commercial exploitation?

(Pages 9 to 15)

EVOLVING YOUR OWN MONEY-MAKING IDEAS

- Would you research: offline, online or both?

- What about hobbies: could one of them be a retirement earner?

- Do you appreciate it's best to make money from what you love doing?

- How many popular retirement hobby earners can you list?

- Would you consider creating opportunities from other people's ideas?

- Do you know the format for listing the things you want to improve?

- What do you know about protecting your ideas?

- What's the best way to generate multiple ideas?

- What benefits accrue from observing everyday things and details?

- Are you aware of any wacky ideas that could make you money?

- What must you do before you start developing your own unusual ideas?

(Pages 16 to 29)

CREATING RESIDUAL INCOME STREAMS

- Why is it restrictive to create residual income offline?

- Why are there more opportunities online?

- What causes countless millions to become hooked on the internet?

- Would you market your own information products?

- Would you choose instead to market other people's produce?

(Pages 30 to 34)

STARTING AN OFFLINE BUSINESS IN RETIREMENT

- How strong is your commitment?

- Would you be capable of making your own decisions?

- Could you plan ahead to cope in all kinds of weather?

- Do you possess good interpersonal skills?

- Will your spouse/partner support your decision?

- Can you afford to invest in yourself?

- How are you at handling setbacks?

- What about the financial side of matters?

- Are you ready to capitalise on major change?

- Do you have special skills?

- Where would you look for help with initial planning?

- How would you set about finding and evaluating ideas?

- What is the formula for evaluating a specific business you have in mind?

- Do you know how to fine tune the selection process?

- Why is it vital to test market when you settle on an idea?

- How does research iron out the wrinkles?

- Are you familiar with the nuts and bolts of running an offline business?

- Do you know how to create your business plan?

- Do you know how to decide the business status for your venture?

- What must you consider when choosing a trading name?

- How would you finance an offline business?

- Why is it vital to find the right location?

- How would you organise affairs before you start?

- Do you understand the basics of accounting and cash flow?

- How would you allow for taxation?

- Are your computer and communication skills up to speed?

- Are you confident about marketing your enterprise?

- Do you know how to acquire commercial skills online?

- Would you add to your skills offline?

- Which crucial questions should you ask your professional advisers?

(Pages 35 to 57)

CHOOSING ONLINE AS THE ROUTE FOR YOUR VENTURE

- Why is online the faster, easier, less stressful route to take?

- Why is it possible to trim start-up costs to the bare minimum?

- Are you comfortable about the flexibility in setting working hours?

- How does your website take orders while you sleep?

- Why is it always 365 day non-stop trading in cyberspace?

- Do you appreciate how your virtual store does business internationally?

- Do you know why you will compete with the moguls on equal terms?

- Do you know why automatic ordering eases the strain?

- Do you know why automatic processing gets the cash in fast?

- Do you know why delivering e-produce instantly creates goodwill?

- Do you know why customer satisfaction means more sales?

- Do you know why virtual customer interfacing reduces stress?

- Do you know the six ways you'll save on operating costs?

- Do you know how to create passive income online?

(Pages 58 to 64)

CREATING PASSIVE INCOME IN CYBERSPACE

- Could you become a master of the unexpected?

- How does giving it all away for free make you money?

- Would you simulate the postal bargains technique?

- Do you know how it works?

- Where would you find sources of supply?

- Do you know what's in it for you?

- Do you know what's required of you?

- Would you join an online forum or discussion group?

- Why is it good practice to check out consumer review websites?

- Would you join an affiliate programme?

- Would you undertake an email survey using your own customer base?

(Pages 65 to 73)

USING YOUR COMPUTER TO MAKE MONEY

- Are you aware you can make money from other people's know-how?

- How would you set up and operate a cyberspace ad agency?

- Could you become clip art specialist?

- Could you offer a home-based desktop publishing service?

- Would you consider creating, registering, auctioning off domain names?

- Could you provide a product endorsement service?

- Could you provide niche solutions for other users?

- Would you share information on your own discussion board?

- Could you develop tools to simplify online tasks?

- Would you open up your site as a training centre?

- Could you compile resources and sell access to the list?

- Could you create an exclusive ezine article centre?

- Do you know how to charge for access to your referrals directory?

- Could you provide an information-on-demand service?

- Could you offer an electronic press release service?

- Could you create a search engine positioning service?

- Could you operate a key phrase discovery service?

- Could you set up as a web graphics designer/copywriter?

- Could you cash in on the latest electronic boom?

- Could you offer creative tuition?

(Pages 74 to 93)

EARNING CASH BY EXPRESSING YOUR OPINIONS

- Do you know how to do it?

- How could you find out more information?

- Could you create multiple income streams from the exercise?

(Pages 94 to 100)

USING RETIREMENT AS THE KEY TO A PROFITABLE PURSUIT

- Would you consider becoming a retirement coaching expert?

- Do you know the benefits accruing from teaching retirement planning?

- Can you define the marketplace?

(Pages 101 to 106)

USING EBAY TO MAKE MONEY BUYING AND SELLING

- How could you gain an edge on online auction competitors?

- What are the essentials for getting started?

- How would you decide what to sell on eBay?

- How would you find your niche market?

- How would you choose an appropriate category?

- Do you know how to keep track of your auctions?

- Do you know why product images are so important on eBay?

- Could you develop a sales strategy?

- Could you project your strategy into the future?

- How would you test your strategy before you start?

- Would you 'feature' your produce?
- Do you know how to access merchandise to sell on eBay?
- Where would you look for tools to help you build your auction business?

(Pages 107 to 117)

OPTING FOR AFFILIATE RESELLING IN RETIREMENT

- What is affiliate reselling?
- What are the benefits of participation?
- How does affiliate reselling work in practice?
- Do you know why MLM isn't a dirty word on the internet?
- Do you know how to undertake an objective overview?
- Why is it best to cast the net wide to begin with?
- What happens if you decide to specialise straightaway?
- How would you go about learning from the competition?
- How would you maintain your essential records?
- What are the steps and stairs to affiliate reselling?
- Do you know where to get a multi-reseller web business for free?

(Pages 118 to 136)

MAKING NICHE MARKETING WORK FOR YOU

- Why did the major dot coms fail?
- Why do most online businesses fail before they even begin?
- What is it that people want most from the internet?
- How did niche marketing spawn a 50-year career for Joe Loss?

- How would you identify an easy-to-target niche market?
- Do you know how to find a product or service that people want?
- How would you test the potential for your niche market?
- Do you know of a tool that provides the answers?
- How would you know if you've struck it niche?
- Could you develop a great sales process?
- Do you know the secrets to unlocking essential core niche factors?

(Pages 137 to 147)

PROMOTING YOUR PRODUCE ONLINE

- Which key factors combine to guarantee effective online promotion?
- What do you know about choosing a domain name?
- Could you build a website to generate sales?
- Could you create interesting content for your pages?
- What's the secret to devising powerful keywords?
- Would you consider using 'smart' pages?
- What are the options for attracting traffic to your site?
- How would you test market before pressing the button?
- Would you use e-books to promote and sell your produce?
- Would you write articles to lure visitors to your website?
- What do you know about linking to other websites?
- What do you know about email marketing?
- Would you create your own newsletter?
- Would you build a list of prospects?

- Would you accept credit cards and online cheques?
- Do you know any other building blocks for attracting customers?

(Pages 151 to 158)

CHOOSING A DOMAIN NAME FOR YOUR VENTURE

- Why is it essential to have your own specific domain name?
- Does it help if it's linked to your produce?
- Why does it help?

(Pages 159 to 164)

CHOOSING THE FORMAT FOR YOUR WEBSITE

- How would you compare mini- and maxi-websites?
- Which is the perfect vehicle for e-books and software?
- Can you describe the advertorial nature of a mini-site?
- Do you know the basic components of an online sales letter?
- Where would you access all-in-one software?
- What is the perfect hosting service for your mini-sites?
- Do you know how a single mini-site can spawn 100s more?
- What do you need when you use the multi-page approach?
- Where would you find the ideal solution for the maxi approach?
- Do you know why designing a 'helpful' site can kill product sales?

(Pages 165 to 177)

USING KEYWORDS TO PROMOTE ONLINE

- How does targeting the right keywords skyrocket your traffic?
- How do people conduct keyword searches?
- Why does targeting *niche* keywords bring instant results?
- Which programme helped generate 839 top spots?
- How do keywords impact on sales?
- Where would you locate free tools to devise powerful keywords?

(Pages 178 to 182)

CREATING CONTENT-RICH PAGES

- Why do words, not graphics, make interesting content?
- Do you reckon this is all new to you?
- So what's different about writing web copy?
- Which 17 vital factors point the way to good web writing?
- How would you encourage interaction with the reader?
- Why does lacing the text with keywords entice the spiders?

(Pages 183 to 188)

USING 'SMART' PAGES

- What exactly are 'smart' pages?
- How difficult are they to create?
- Which tool claims to have all the answers?
- Are smart pages as clever as they're cracked up to be?
- Can you name alternative software for generating smart pages?

(Pages 189 to 192)

AVOIDING SEARCH ENGINE POSITIONING MISTAKES

- What happens when you optimise your site for the wrong keywords?

- What happens when you put too many keywords in the Meta Tag?

- What happens when you repeat the same keyword too many times?

- What do you understand by the term 'hidden text'?

- Why does creating pages containing only graphics weaken positioning?

- When would you use page cloaking?

- Why is using automatic submission software inadvisable?

- Why is submitting too many pages daily a bad practice?

- Why is spending too much time on search engine positioning counter productive?

(Pages 193 to 198)

FLOODING YOUR SITE WITH TRAFFIC

- What do you know about pay-per-click (PPC) search engines?

- Would you go for newsgroup, forum, ad mailing list participation?

- Would you trade links with other websites?

- Would you write articles for ezines and magazines?

- Would you use CGI traffic plug-ins on your site?

- Would you use the power of free press releases?

(Pages 199 to 203)

TEST-MARKETING EVERY TASK

- Are you investing or gambling in your niche retirement opportunity?

- How would you determine how much to spend on website visitors?

- What does adding up your income and unique visitors tell you?

- How would you set up a website tracking system?

- Would you use a free counter for each page?

- Would you install a CGI program to track your stats?

- Would you purchase your domain where stats are part of the deal?

- How would you key all your promotional efforts?

- How would you judge results to expand your promotion?

(Pages 204 to 210)

USING DIGITISED BOOKS

- Do you know how to create your own digital information produce?

- Can you create virtual book covers automatically?

- Have you devised the strategy for sales and distribution?

- Why does it pay to give e-books away for free?

- Would you choose to sell someone else's produce?

(Pages 211 to 217)

EXPLOITING THE POWER OF ARTICLES

- Where would you start?

- Are you now confident about writing your first article for distribution?

- What is the worst case scenario for published articles?

- Do you know where to submit your article output for free?

- Which software does it all automatically?

- Would you use press releases for distribution?

(Pages 218 to 224)

LINKING TO OTHER WEBSITES

- Are you familiar with the 10 easy steps for building link popularity?

- Do you know why reciprocal linking increases website effectiveness?

- How does combining articles and links create a traffic virus?

(Pages 225 to 233)

UNDERSTANDING EMAIL MARKETING

- What is the vital difference between bulk email and opt-in email?

- What are the myths surrounding opt-in email?

- What 12 common email mistakes must you always avoid?

- Do you know the five ways to earn more using email?

(Pages 234 to 245)

CREATING YOUR OWN NEWSLETTER

- Which common goals do all newsletter publishers share?

- Which two secrets convert your ezine into a cash machine?

(Pages 246 to 251)

BUILDING OPT-IN LISTS

- What are the secrets to building massive opt-in lists?

(Pages 252 to 256)

CONVERTING PROSPECTS

- Can you name the 10 reasons why people buy?
- What is the golden rule of selling?

(Pages 257 to 260)

ACCEPTING CREDIT CARDS

- Can you name the consumer fears on disclosing credit card information?

(Pages 261 to 266)

POINTING AND CLICKING YOUR WAY TO PROFITS

- What do know about Marlon Sanders' *Marketing Dashboard*?
- What do you know about Michael Green's *How to Promote a Product*?

(Pages 267 to 271)

THE FUTURE OF ONLINE TRADING

Have you studied the questions raised in *378 Internet Marketing Predictions*?

FINAL WORDS

'And now our revels are over'

William Shakespeare

And now *you know everything I know* about finding a profitable retirement pursuit. If you are of a mind to join those countless retirees who have already rejected conventional retirement, then go for it, and without delay. It will be the beginning of a grand third age adventure.

I shall take my leave of you with these final words:

- Chase the money and you will probably fail.

- Choose fulfilment and the money is certain to follow.

Good luck.

Glossary

Affiliate reselling	Virtual sales agency; pays out commissions on referral sales.
Automatic payment processing	Electronic system; completes transactions from secure server and fulfils orders automatically.
Content-rich webpage	Web page copy interlaced with keywords to attract the search engine 'spiders'.
Digital produce	Produce such as informational merchandise and software that is digitised and marketed online.
Directory listing	Having a website catalogued in the major online registers such as Google, Yahoo!, Zeal, etc.
Discussion board	Electronic notice board where visitors can post messages and items of interest to other online users.
Domain name	The URL (uniform resource locator) or address for a website.
Dropshipping	Wholesale system whereby the buyer draws down on demand individual items of merchandise for resale. Wholesaler delivers goods direct to customer then bills buyer.
E-book	Transcript that is manufactured in digital format; such as book, document, article, etc.
E-commerce	The practice of buying and selling online.
Email marketing	Promoting merchandise online using email as the vehicle for relaying sales messages to prospective buyers.
Email survey	Conducting an online survey using email.
Ezine	An electronic newsletter.

292

FTP **(File Transfer Protocol)**	System for uploading files from one website to another.
Google.com	The leading online search engine.
'Hollow' operation	Refers to a business where everything is outsourced, meaning you would subcontract manufacturing and packaging to outside sources.
Information product	Generally ascribed to informational produce that has been digitally manufactured for resale or to be given away online.
Internet ad agency	Online advertising agency designed to assist users in website construction and maintenance.
Keyword	Core word that is included in web page text as an aid to defining overall context.
Keyword phrase	Key words paired together to achieve same result.
Limited company	A company limited by law in the transaction of business.
Link popularity	The extent as measured by the quality of its text links to other websites to which a website is favoured by search engines and users alike.
Links and banners	Text links and image banners which interact electronically with other websites.
List building	The process of building a list of prospective customers or parties interested in an online marketing proposition.
Multi-level marketing	Cyclical selling; selling system with many layers attached to it; similar to the steps in an escalator: what goes down invariably comes back up.
Multi-dimensional website	A website consisting of multiple pages of diverse data.
Multiple income streams	The process of developing a string of online money-making opportunities.

NewDeal 50Plus	The government agency that can assist retirees in growing a part-time business proposition.
Niche	Tiny but popular markets, produce, customer classifications.
Offline business	Any business that conducts its affairs without using the internet.
One-page website	A website consisting of a single page.
Online auctions	Auctions conducted solely on the internet.
Online forum	An online meeting place for enthusiasts on a given topic.
Online research	Research undertaken using internet facilities.
Online survey	Market or consumer survey conducted on the internet.
Partnership	A legal arrangement whereby two or more people agree to carry out business with joint and individual responsibilities and liabilities.
Passive income	Income that is generated from a one-time action which continues to produce revenue passively.
Pay-per-click	The process whereby internet users pay a fee to attract visitors to their websites.
PDF (Portable Document Folder)	Captures formatting information from a variety of desktop publishing applications; can be read on any computer anywhere in the world.
Referral fee	Term associated with affiliate reselling where commissions are paid on referred sales.
Retirement coaching	Training pre-retirees on retirement planning.
Search engine positioning	Search engine optimised web pages that drive targeted traffic to websites; also known as gateway or doorway pages.
Search engine 'spiders'	Electronic robots that travel throughout cyberspace assessing website suitability for inclusion in search engine listings.

Small business advisory initiative	Government agency gateway for small businesses.
Smart pages	Device enabling web pages to be replicated many times over; so increasing chances of higher search engine rankings.
Sole trader	Someone who operates a business as sole principal.
Spam blockers	Software to obstruct uninvited email messages arriving in the user's inbox.
Test-marketing	The practice of testing out the potential of a product or service before launching it in the marketplace.
Third age entrepreneur	Retiree businessperson.

Resources

Affiliate reselling

activemarketplace.com

www.clickbank.com

www.marketingtips.com

www.profitsvault.com

www.howtocorp.com

www.sitesell.com/interactive1.html

www.sixfigureincome.com/?122341

www.amazon.com

Article hubs

ezinearticles.com

www.articlehub.com

www.certificate.net/wwio

www.ideamarketers.com

www.marketing-seek.com

www.goarticles.com

www.netterweb.com

www.articlesfactory.com

www.worldabooks.com/writers-connection/

www.web-source.net/syndicator_submit.htm

www.searchwarp.com

www.etext.org

www.zinos.com

www.freelancewriting.com/newssyndicator.html

www.homebasedbusinessindex.com

www.home-based-business-opportunities.com

www.homebusinessuk.co.uk/surfing.htm

www.homeincome.com

www.linksnoop.com

www.addme.com

www.vectorcentral.com

www.webpronews.com

www.press-releases.net

Author's self-help websites

howtoproducts-xl.com

howtoproducts-xl.com/2.html

howtoproducts-xl.com/ccc.html

howtoproducts-xl.com/madhatter.html

howtoproducts-xl.com/niche.html

1st-creative-writing-course.com

1st-creative-writing-course.com/gettingpublished.html

1st-creative-writing-course.com/homeshopoffice/online.html

1st-creative-writing-course.com/makemoney.html

1st-creative-writing-course.com/mistakes/acm.html

1st-creative-writing-course.com/progress/pro.html

1st-creative-writing-course.com/starting/starting.html

1st-creative-writing-course.com/wfp.html

costcutters.howtoproducts-xl.com

makingmoneyonline-xl.com

retirement-moneymakers.com

start-a-business-masterplan.com

Auto-responders

www.aweber.com

www.getresponse.com

www.autobots.net

www.autoresponders.com

www.freeautobot.com

www.ultimateresponse.com

Consumer reviews

www.consumerreview.com

www.consumersearch.com

www.consumersdigest.com

Digital book creators

www.ebookcovergenerator.com

www.ebookgenerator.com

www.adobe.com

www.docudesk.com/

Doing online surveys for cash

www.easytorecall.com/online_surveys.htm

www.apennyearned.co.uk/surveys_uk.html

www.getpaidguides.com/survey/companies.html

Domain names

www.OpenForSale.com

www.whois.com

E-book cover generator

www.virtualcovercreator.com

Ezines

www.ezineaction.com

www.ezineadvertising.com

www.ezine-dir.com

www.ezinelocater.com

www.ezine-marketing.com

www.ezinesearch.com

www.ezinestoday.com

www.ezinearticles.com

www.new-list.com

Keyword selection

www.goodkeywords.com

inventory.overture.com/d/searchinventory/suggestion/

Offline business planning

www.clearlybusiness.com

www.myownbusiness.org

www.coursepal.com

Online auctions

www.auctionsniper.com

www.usnetnews.com/ebay/index.cgi?trffxeb2142

pages.ebay.co.uk/ebay_toolbar/index.html

pages.ebay.co.uk/turbo_lister/download.html

Online credit card processors

www.clickbank.com

www.paypal.com

Online discussion groups

www.groups.google.com

www.talkcity.com

www.insidetheweb.com

www.forumone.com

www.searchengineforums.com/bin/Ultimate.cgi

Retirement coaching

www.retirementoptions.com

Smart pages

www.smartpagecreator.com

www.smartpagegenerator.com

www.smartpagepro.com

www.the-whole-truth.com

Spam filter

http://spamcheck.sitesell.com

Using your computer to make money

www.yourmembershipwebsite.com/

www.thewarriorgroup.com

www.timeblaster.com/tbeindex.shtml

www.tunza-products.com/classified/ads.html

www.universalthread.com

www.discusware.com

www.kikamoocow.worldonline.co.uk/freecash.htm

www.leads4insurance.com

www.angieslist.com

www.AssociatePrograms.com

www.bigplaystocks.com

www.abundancecenter.com

ultimateadvertisingclub.com

Web hosting

www.sitesell.com/interactive1.html

thirdspherehosting.com/plus/?xstcreat&id=xstcreat&pkg=

www.hosting.com

Useful reading

43 Ways to Make Money Online, Joe Vitale, Jo Han Mock (John Wiley & Sons 2005)

Developing Your Online Business Profitability, Martin Brighty, Dean Markham (Spiro Press 2003)

Little E, Big Commerce: How to Make a Profit Online, Sir Richard Branson (Foreword), Timothy Cumming (Virgin Books 2001)

Starting an Online Business for Dummies, Greg Holden (Hungry Minds Inc, 2002)

Small Business Websites That Work, Sean McManus (Prentice Hall 2003)

The Complete Idiot's Guide to Starting a Business Online, Frank Fiore (Que 2000)

The Online Copywriter's Handbook: *Everything You Need to Know to Write Electronic Copy That Sells*, Robert W. Bly (Contemporary Books 2003)

Multiple Streams of Internet Income: *How Ordinary People Make Extraordinary Money Online*, Robert Allen (John Wiley & Sons Inc 2002)

New Ideas About New Ideas: *Insights on Creativity from the World's Leading Innovators*, Shira P. White, G.Patton Wright (Financial Times Prentice Hall 2002)

Why They Don't Buy: *Make Your Online Customer Experience Work,*
Max Mckeown, (Financial Times Prentice Hall 2001)

Starting an Internet Business at Home, Jim Green, (Kogan Page 2001)

*Starting Your Own Business: The Bestselling Guide to Planning and
Building a Successful Enterprise*, Jim Green (How To Books 2005)

Index